MILITARY CAMOUFLAGE

BERNARD LOWRY

AMBERLEY

To Geraldine

First published 2023

Amberley Publishing
The Hill, Stroud,
Gloucestershire, GL5 4EP

www.amberley-books.com

ISBN: 978 1 3981 0860 8 (print)
ISBN: 978 1 3981 0861 5 (ebook)

British Library Cataloguing in Publication Data.
A catalogue record for this book is available from the British Library.

Typeset in 10pt on 13pt Celeste.
Typesetting by SJmagic DESIGN SERVICES, India.
Printed in the UK.

Contents

Introduction

The word 'camouflage' has its origins in the French word *camoufler*, meaning to hide or conceal. Concealment is seen in nature where it bestows an advantage on hunter and hunted alike. In military use it has been defined as any artificial means employed to deceive the enemy's visual or photographic observation from the ground or from the air. Concealment of a shape or outline can be achieved by blending it with its background, ensuring that tone, texture, regularity and colour match and that shine is avoided. A good example of this in nature is the polar bear, which is white to match its surroundings. There are some basic considerations: the avoidance of shadows by using countershading (where the underside of an object is lightened to minimise shadow effect), or by the darkening of light areas and the lightening of darker areas; for example, those unavoidably in shadow. However, where detection is unavoidable, the use of designs that confuse the eye and so delay recognition can be employed.

Historically, camouflage has been seen to bestow a military advantage. Caesar is said to have painted the sails of a number of his ships, engaged on reconnaissance, so that they would blend with the sea. In Edward I's campaign in Wales, after the capture of the Welsh castle of Dolwyddelan in January 1283 he took immediate steps to equip the garrison for winter warfare by ordering his tailor, Robert, to supply 80 yards of white material for camouflage clothing, possibly Irish linen, plus fifty-seven pairs of white stockings to be sent from the campaign base at Chester. In literature, Shakespeare's *Macbeth* has Malcolm's army before Macbeth's castle at Inverness carrying natural camouflage: 'Now near enough; your leafy screens throw down.'

In the nineteenth century the brightly coloured uniforms of the past were being seen as a liability given the changing nature of warfare, with, for example, the provision of more efficient, longer-ranging rifles. With set-piece battles, where it was necessary for friend and foe to be identified by their uniforms, no longer the mode, there was a move towards more efficient uniforms. In the British army green uniforms, worn by certain units, began to make an appearance from the beginning of the nineteenth century, made famous by the fictional character of the sharpshooting rifleman Sharpe in the eponymous TV series. Henceforth, green would be the colour of the uniforms of the Rifle Corps regiments. The exception to this trend was France, whose army uniforms

An example of natural camouflage: the butterfly *kallima inachus,* the under surfaces of its wings replicating a dead leaf on a forest floor.

remained into the beginning of the First World War very much as they appeared in the 1870 Franco-Prussian War. This consisted of a dark blue jacket and red trousers. The French cavalry combined this with large plumed and shiny metal helmets not unlike those seen worn by knights in the Middle Ages.

A revolutionary change in the appearance of uniforms came with the invention of the khaki dye, which was initially a light shade. Soldiers of the East India Company are said to have resorted to covering their bright uniforms in mud to give them an advantage when fighting tribal armies. A suitable dye was called for and this appeared in the mid-nineteenth century, using the minerals chrome and iron oxide, which on drying produced a colour-fast

The striking difference between the appearance of the French soldier of 1914 (left) and the new *horizon bleu* uniform.

dye to produce khaki, an Indian word for dust. The British army first used the colour in action during the Boer Wars of 1880–1902. In John Galsworthy's great saga Soames Forsyte's mother speaks approvingly of her grandson's new khaki uniform as he is about to sail for South Africa. A darker shade of the colour, with good concealment properties in temperate climates, was introduced for the British army, and this was copied by many armies in the twentieth century. Of the other major warring nations Italy and Germany both used a grey-green colour. The United States adopted khaki, calling it Olive Drab. In the twentieth century the practice of camouflage became extensive and highly developed with the use of artists, scientists, naturalists and other specialists, as we shall see. Developments in chemical dyes led to further sophistication as well.

PLAYER'S CIGARETTES

THE LOVAT SCOUTS, 1900

A 1938 cigarette card showing a British soldier in South Africa wearing the newly introduced light khaki uniform. (Courtesy of Imperial Tobacco)

1

The First World War

The commencement of the First World War saw aircraft overflying the enemy's positions and reporting back to military headquarters with their observations. The first successful use of aerial reconnaissance was during the battle of Tannenburg on Germany's eastern front on 30 August 1914, after which victory Field Marshal Hindenburg declared, 'Without German aviation there would have been no Tannenburg.' The allies were not far behind. On 3 September a French Breguet aircraft reported that the invading German army had changed course, intelligence that led to the critical first battle of the Marne a few days later. Work carried out by BE2s of the British Expeditionary Force convinced the British commander in chief, General French, of the value of aerial observation. From then the pace accelerated. Photographic reconnaissance aircraft, becoming ever more sophisticated, could fly at over 18,000 feet – beyond the range of enemy anti-aircraft guns. Close to front lines artillery-spotting tethered balloons observed the enemy's movements. On the ground the smallest degree of elevation was critical and both sides made use of artificial trees, church towers and converted ruins as observation posts. Clearly, screening and camouflage were called for, the British using screens of coconut matting or nets with scrim (strips of dyed hessian) to hide all signs of movement from enemy observation including snipers. Larger objects such as artillery pieces were hidden under nets, camouflage painted or moved into covered pits.

Uniforms

Although the French infantryman had begun the war in colourful red and blue uniforms, France had been developing a new uniform colour called *tricolore*, a mixture of the national colours of red, white and blue, producing a dark bluish grey colour with superior camouflage value. However, the advent of war deprived France of the necessary red dye, to be procured from Germany, which had an advanced chemical dye industry, so cloth was obtained from Britain in a grey blue shade called *gris angleterre*. This temporary expedient was replaced towards the end of 1914 by French manufactured cloth in a colour known as *horizon bleu*. Too light in colour for the mud of northern and eastern France it served throughout the war and remained in limited use by second line troops until the beginning of the Second World War, being replaced by a greenish khaki (*kaki*) between the wars. In fact, a light shade of khaki was already in use by the country's colonial troops, large numbers of these men being sent to the European fighting. In mountainous areas France, like Germany and Austria-Hungary, made use of snow camouflage suits for skiers patrolling in winter. A modern-looking reversible grey/white *windjacke* was introduced for ski troops by the latter two countries. France would also, like the other major combatants, make use of extempore camouflaged sniper suits,

Germany's troops wore grey-green (*feldgrau*) uniform jackets and slate grey trousers. Their early protective helmets of leather were supplied with a cover in light khaki from 1892 onwards to mask and protect the prominent regimental badge displayed on the front, the cover often being stamped with the regimental number. From 1916 troops began to be issued with a distinctive steel helmet painted in *feldgrau* but often camouflaged with black-bordered patches of colour, in an attempt to break up the helmet's prominent outline. Britain, of course, used khaki. The soldiers' steel helmets, with a tendency to shine, were supplied with cloth covers but there were probably never enough of these, the Tommy's helmet more often is seen camouflaged by a cover made from sacking. One item of clothing unique to the British army was the kilt cover in khaki material designed to both protect the kilt aid as an aid to camouflaging the brighter tartans. Apart from a small contingent of Marines, who used Forest Green, the USA continued to use Olive Drab for army uniforms and equipment.

Aircraft

British aircraft began the war, as other countries, with their linen fabric covering painted in a clear cellulose varnish (known as dope) – this gave good concealment from below or in the air, against the sky. The need for concealment from above by reconnaissance aircraft while on the ground or by fighter aircraft resulted in the introduction of a dull khaki brown dope for all upper surfaces called PC.10. This had been produced to a Royal Aircraft Factory specification, the lower surfaces of wings and tailplanes being clear doped with V.114, another official varnish. On entry into the war in 1917 the USA lacked a developed military aircraft industry and was forced to build suitable allied aircraft under licence or to purchase them outright – the former were finished in Olive Drab while the latter retained the camouflage finish of the country of origin. Among these were large numbers of French aircraft. France introduced camouflage for its aircraft in 1918, which consisted of a disruptive pattern of varying tones of green and brown on upper surfaces, with the addition of irregular patches of black on horizontal surfaces. However, this was often compromised by large and bright personal or squadron markings reflecting the Gallic *joie de vivre*.

Germany's aircraft generally left the factories in the manufacturer's chosen finish. For example, early Pfalz aircraft were painted in silver dope, while Fokker aircraft received a streaky olive green finish (unless you were the Red Baron!). The wooden fuselages of Albatros aircraft were varnished, the upper portions of wings and tailplanes being painted in bands of green and mauve, or pale Brunswick green, Venetian brown and olive green,

In France's aviation museum in Paris is this Breguet 14 XIV reconnaissance bomber painted in a disruptive pattern.

A fragment of original German lozenge fabric from the fuselage of a 1918 AEG JII ground attack aircraft in colours appropriate to its role.

with the under surfaces doped pale blue. Later in the war a degree of standardisation was introduced, with aircraft leaving the factories covered in pre-printed linen cloth in a four- or five-colour lozenge pattern, resulting in a time bonus as only varnishing was required. The colours varied according to the mission of the aircraft, and the colours printed onto the linen used for lower surfaces was always in lighter colours than that used for the upper surfaces. An examination of a surviving example of the upper-surface five-colour lozenge material of a fighter aircraft identified contrasting colours: blue black, purple grey, khaki yellow, sage green, and dark cobalt blue. Lower surface colours were light turquoise, dark mauve, golden yellow, pink-purple, and blue-grey. On the other hand, night bombing aircraft lozenge material printed in black, blues and greys. Aircraft manufactured by Germany's ally Austria-Hungary were also to be seen in a variation of the lozenge-printed material, but in colours different to those of Germany's and in a more regular pattern. Finally, an experiment to make a German aircraft almost invisible in the air failed dismally. The Linke-Hofman R.1 bomber had its rear fuselage completely covered in Cellon, a type of clear celluloid. However, the intense reflective properties of the material made the aircraft more visible! It was also found that sunlight turned the Cellon yellow and shrank, affecting the control of the aircraft. Eventually this large and unsuccessful aircraft was covered in lozenge material, the whale-like aircraft requiring large quantities of the material.

Modern lozenge fabric used in the restoration of a German First World War reconnaissance aircraft.

However, Germany's attempts at aircraft concealment, at least as far as fighter aircraft are concerned, were often compromised by the large black and white cross, national marking, and by the often brightly painted, personal markings of its pilots, which in an aerial battle aided identification. Such a practice was anathema to the British.

Military Vehicles

The first British tank, the Mk 1, was initially painted in a variety of concealment designs drawn up by the artist Solomon Solomon, including one involving a patchwork of colours, another featuring stripes of ochre, red-brown and green, while another used grey, green, brown and ochre with narrow, vegetal black stripes separating the colours. Camouflage was thought essential to disguise the tank's large and high rhomboidal shape. However, no camouflage could disguise the noise of the early tanks, and in any event the tank's camouflage soon became covered in the mud of the Western Front, itself an effective camouflage. These elaborate schemes were soon abandoned in place of an overall and simple brown colour. Royal Naval Air Service Rolls-Royce armoured cars, operating on roads, were given, appropriately, a coat of battleship grey. The smaller and nimbler French FT17 tanks were given vertical stripes in greens and browns, often outlined in black. No laid down scheme appears to have prevailed: the designs being painted at the whim of the

A captured British Mk IV tank on the Western Front. Mechanically unreliable, a number were captured by Germany in December 1917 and put back into use against their former owners. Black identification crosses overlie the original patchwork camouflage.

A restored French Renault FT17 tank showing the appearance of these machines in the First World War and in the immediate post-war period.

factory painter. The large and clumsy St Chamond tank was given a segmental scheme of ochre, burnt sienna, green and cream outlined in black. France relied on large numbers of lorries to supply the Verdun sector and these were camouflaged against aerial observation, at least one scheme being in an overtly Cubist style.

Germany's small number of A7V tanks were given diffuse patches of chestnut and dark green over an ochre base.

Artillery

The British established in France a Special Works Park in 1916 to make camouflaged observation posts; for example, in the form of false trees, made hollow to take an observer. French women were employed to tie the strips of hessian (scrim) onto nets for the vast quantities of camouflage netting required on the Western Front to obscure guns, ammunition dumps and headquarters from aerial observation. In September 1917, US forces established a Camouflage Section in France.

The Western Front developed into a war of the guns with ever heavier calibres being employed. Such large weapons were difficult to conceal from aerial observation, whether by aircraft or balloon, so much effort was put into their concealment. Their muzzle blast created problems, too, moving or even setting fire to jute camouflage nets, so, if available, metal netting was sought. French artillery at the start of the war was painted a

A model of a British fabricated observation tree as used on the Western Front.

14

uniform medium grey. Guns, drawn by teams of horses, would, it was planned, be rushed to whichever part of a battlefield they were required and camouflage was secondary. However, the onset of static warfare with heavier and heavier calibres of gun together with the constant threat of aerial observation led the French to employ artists to design camouflage schemes. Artists (known as *camoufleurs*) under the direction of Guirand de Scévola were sent to the front to camouflage the guns; he claimed that in order to disguise the aspect of an object it was firstly necessary to employ the means that the cubists used to represent it. New weapons now began to leave the factories in camouflage. One artist, André Mare, a founder of the Art Deco movement, who belonged to a French camouflage section, sketched in 1916 (his sketchbook survives) on the Somme front a scheme for a 280-mm Schneider howitzer. This broke up the shape of the gun using the grey base colour together with patches of burnt sienna, dark green and ochre, with black lines separating the colours. The use of camouflage painting had become widespread in the French army from 1915 onwards. Other schemes used soft-edged patches of colour or spots of colour in a *pointilliste* manner. A French army manual of 1917 specified matte colours in shades of ochre, green and with black divisions. Large patches of colour were to be applied irregularly with black lines separating the colours: the manual stated that, so painted, an object was invisible even at a short distance, its outline effectively broken up. A surviving 155-mm Baquet artillery piece in the Brussels Royal Museum of the Armed Forces and Military History retains its original colours of dark green, rust brown and yellow ochre, the colours separated by prominent black lines. An additional colour is believed to have been used by France, *vert d'eau* (sea green). The colours established in the war would be reintroduced when France modernised its armour in the late 1930s.

Germany also made use of camouflage to disguise its artillery. The artist Franz Marc, a founder of the *Blaue Reiter* school and a cavalryman in the Imperial German Army, was drafted in 1916 into a military camouflage section. His brief was to design a quantity of gun covers, and to do this he tried to visualise how these might appear from an aircraft 2,000 feet high. Too good a challenge for an artist, he painted them, apparently, in the styles of famous artists ranging from Monet to Kandinsky. Before he could be officially commissioned as a war artist, however, Marc was killed at Verdun in 1916. In addition to passive camouflage, the careful masking of planned operations could reap dividends. In April 1918, Germany used careful camouflaging to conceal the Ludendorff offensive against French positions on the *Chemin des Dames*. The French were caught unawares. General Allenby in Arabia also successfully used deception techniques against the Turks in 1917. However, after the end of the war the art of deception was largely forgotten.

Defence Installations

The camouflaging of important British military assets had begun before the outbreak of war. Flagstaff Battery in Colombo, Ceylon, had a tall battery control post built to resemble a civilian building, complete with balconies and arched windows. The 10-inch guns of Stonecutters West Battery protecting the naval base of Hong Kong had their barrels painted with a disruptive pattern. The overflying of Britain by Zeppelins and German bombers led to the camouflage of some strategic buildings; for example, the large airship hangers at Cardington in Bedfordshire were given a disruptive camouflage scheme. The occupation of Belgium left Germany close to Britain and there was a fear of invasion. Defences were erected along the country's south-east and eastern coasts. Camouflage was used to obscure these works; for example, at Sheerness in Kent a battery of 4.7-inch guns mounted on towers were camouflaged in a disruptive jigsaw pattern. Another battery of 15-pdr guns on the Isle of Sheppey at Merryman's Hill were camouflaged as large beach huts. The shadow shading of large coastal artillery pieces, a method also adopted by the Royal Navy, was undertaken. This involved the painting of the undersides of these large guns in a light colour, so alleviating the tell-tale shadows seen under gun barrels.

Warships

At the start of the war the British Admiralty displayed little interest in camouflage; apart from destroyers painted black for dusk operations, the country's warships were painted grey. The launch of the German U-boat campaign at the beginning of the war and mounting losses in shipping prompted a call for research into the better concealment of ships. A pattern known as Dazzle camouflage was devised not to make a ship invisible but to break up its form, thereby making it difficult for a submarine to determine a vessel's exact course and so complicate range finding, leading to a torpedo 'miss'. The first ships to be 'Dazzled' were fifty vulnerable troopships. The scheme was had been influenced by earlier work by the American naturalist and artist Abbott Thayer and the British zoologist Graham Kerr – it was the application of nature to war. However, the driving force behind the painting of the 'Dazzle' ships was the marine artist and naval officer Norman Wilkinson. Beginning in 1917 over 4,000 merchant ships and 400 warships were given Dazzle camouflage and

The aircraft carrier HMS *Argus* wearing its Dazzle scheme.

Norman Wilkinson's striking Dazzle scheme for RMS *Mauretania.*

the practice was also adopted by the USA. A Dazzle section was established in Burlington House in London of artists and Admiralty officials to draw up suitable designs – sloping lines, curves, and stripes were used. Other designs included diamond shapes evoking the cubist movement – the troop transport RMS *Mauretania* was given such a scheme by Wilkinson. At the ports and dockyards, artist officers such as Edward Wadsworth, a vorticist, supervised the painting according to the drawings given to them. Wadsworth, who would later in the war be sent to the USA to set up a 'Dazzle' section, in his later woodcuts turned 'Dazzle' into art. The camouflage was not universally appreciated as many naval officers felt the painting made their ships look garish and sloppy. In one instance, in reply to such a reaction, a Camouflage Officer pointed out that the object of camouflage was not to make a ship resemble a West African parrot but rather to give the impression that 'your head is where your stern really is'. Although the schemes had merit, in practice a skilled U- boat commander could deduce direction by following the movements of a ship's masts. Later in the war a school for German submariners was set up at Kiel to specifically counter Dazzle.

Two light colours were generally included in the schemes to emulate the sky, together with contrasting colours such as black, dark blues and greys. It had the disadvantage that in the strong light of the Mediterranean the dark colours tended to stand out, and at night or dusk (the usual time for a U-boat attack) the light colours were prominent. The most important areas for treatment were the stern and forward areas of a ship. After the First World War 'Dazzle' was quickly dropped (although it was reintroduced by the US Navy in the Second World War) for the traditional naval grey, and although the effectiveness of the schemes can be questioned, it probably did help the morale of those who sailed in the 'Dazzle' ships. Germany, less reliant on shipping, largely stuck to a traditional grey colour, but it did adopt tactics to disguise its armed commerce raiders, adding false funnels and hiding guns under covers.

2

Between the Wars

The 'war to end all wars' did not end conflict; there would be fighting after November 1918 in eastern Europe, as we shall see. The nature of warfare would gradually change between the world wars with the disappearance of static trench warfare and set-piece battles. Instead, warfare would become more fluid and fast changing. However, the First World War would still dominate military thinking as witness the construction of the Maginot Line in northern France, a technically advanced and super-expensive Hindenburg Line.

Uniforms

The first item of personal camouflaged equipment appeared in 1929 in Mussolini's Italy. This was a three-colour, rectangular tent section. A number could be buttoned together to form a shelter or be worn as a waterproof cape. Its warm colours of ochre, chestnut and olive green evoked those of the Italian countryside. The three basic colours would also be seen used on Italy's aircraft and tanks. In the latter part of the next war the material would be turned into jackets and trousers to be worn by Italian elite units such as paratroopers or members of the X MAS Flotilla. After the Italian surrender in 1943 large quantities of the cloth were seized by Germany and made into camouflage clothing, predominantly for the Waffen-SS, which because of its extremely high combat loss rate had an insatiable demand for replacement camouflage clothing. Its use was seen most notably among the ranks of the 12.SS-Panzer Division 'Hitler Jugend', especially during the bloody fighting in Normandy in June 1944. The pattern was readopted by Italy after the Second World War. Following Italy's example, in 1938 Hungary introduced a shelter quarter in a similar pattern, but with cream replacing ochre. It should be mentioned here that while personal camouflage protection was of obvious value when a soldier was stationary it had little or no value when its wearer was in motion.

Germany was not slow to follow suit. In 1931, two years before Hitler came to power, the country introduced a triangular, reversible shelter quarter known as the *Zeltbahn*, four of which could be buttoned together to form a small tent, or, individually, could be buttoned across the body as a waterproof and extempore item of camouflage clothing. Reflecting

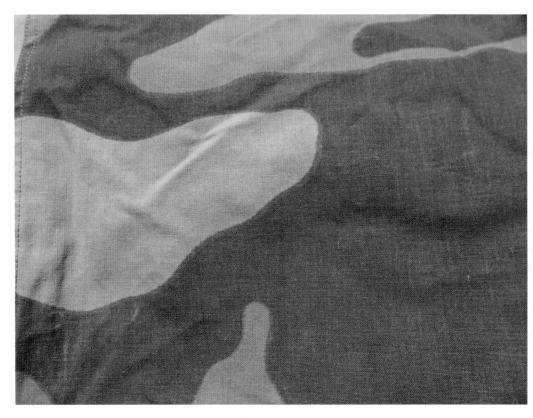

The 1929 Italian camouflage pattern material.

the cool colours of northern Europe, one side of the green and brown splinter pattern had a grey background, the other a light brown background. A rare alternative had one side printed in a brown splinter pattern. In addition to the splinters, a 'rain' pattern was overprinted onto the material to add a degree of diffusion. This motif being was adopted post-war by several Warsaw Pact countries. The geometric pattern of the splinters enabled several shelters to be buttoned together without compromising the camouflage effect of the whole.

The accession of the Nazi Party to power in 1933 and its grip on the state led to the creation of the Waffen-SS, a form of Praetorian Guard. This army within an army would grow enormously during the Second World War. The Waffen-SS did not adopt the Wehrmacht's *Zeltbahn*, which they felt to be unsatisfactory in terms of its camouflage value. Instead, tests were carried out from 1935 by an engineer member of the Waffen-SS, a Dr Brandt, for new and revolutionary items of camouflage clothing, including a reversible camouflage jacket known as the *Tarnjacke* (with loops for the attachment of foliage), intended to be worn over a soldier's personal equipment. In addition, a helmet cover, *Zeltbahn* and face mask were produced before war broke out in 1939. Several reversible patterns were produced under the direction of Professor Otto Schick: black, bright and dark greens and a pink brown for summer, and black, greys and browns for winter. It has been suggested that these were drawn up following Schick's observations on the

Zeltbahn joined together in fours to form shelters in woodland. Their triangular shape and head openings are apparent.

Detail of a *Zeltbahn* showing the seasonal grey and brown backgrounds (lower) together with characteristic 'raindrops'.

passage of sunlight through trees. The SS patterns used groups of colours, sometimes with very diffuse shapes, to give maximum camouflage effect at varying distances, known as the fractal effect – large patterns work well at longer ranges, smaller patterns at closer ranges. The Wehrmacht's splinter pattern was felt to give a poor result at short ranges. The first pattern is believed to be the one known to collectors as the Plane Tree pattern as it resembles the bark of this tree and is believed to have been introduced in 1936. No records have been traced to confirm the original names of these patterns, if they these ever existed. The next pattern introduced in *c.* 1940 is known as the Palm Tree pattern because of its elongated leaf shapes, a pattern soon abandoned. In 1941, a Blurred Edge pattern and an Oakleaf pattern appeared. Late war shortages of high-quality waterproof cotton duck material led to the final SS pattern being introduced, the Dot or Pea pattern,

The short-lived Waffen-SS Palm Tree pattern of long leaf shapes – the spring/summer side is shown.

so named as its pattern used small groups of different colours. In a departure, it was made as a two-piece uniform with pockets in twill material and provided both a working and a combat uniform. An examination by the US army in 1944 of Waffen-SS uniforms judged that they had excellent camouflage properties. The earliest uniforms were block printed by hand, but this system was quickly replaced by machine-operated rollers. It should be noted that the SS had vast resources of forced labour for the manufacture of its uniforms, and research was based at Munich close to the Dachau concentration where abundant forced labour was available.

Camouflage was termed *maskirovka* by the Soviet Union. The country had established in July 1939 a Service for the Camouflaging of the Soviet Forces, although this initially

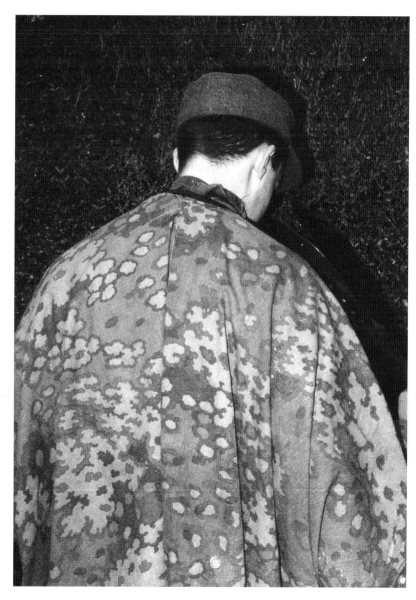

The spring and summer side of a Waffen-SS Oakleaf pattern *Zeltbahn*.

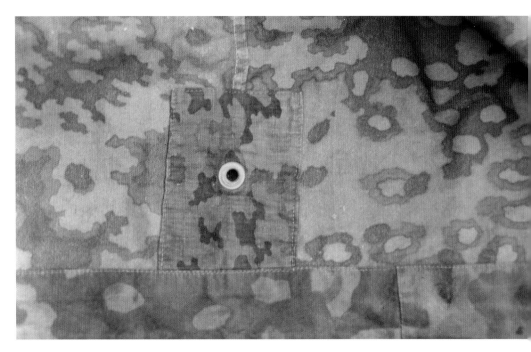

Detail of the autumn and winter sides of a Waffen-SS Oakleaf pattern *Zeltbahn*, also showing a strip of Plane Tree pattern edging (lower).

The Soviet amoeba pattern. Although colorised, the image gives a good impression of this roomy garment, here worn by highly decorated ace sniper Lyudmila Pavlichenko. Her weapon is a Tokarev rifle with telescopic sight.

related to aircraft, but the country had already introduced in 1937 a very roomy, hooded, two-piece camouflage suit with a large, irregular design known to collectors as the MKK or amoeba pattern printed in either a spring/summer pattern of dark brown over green, or dark brown on a light khaki background for the autumn/winter pattern. This would see widespread use in what the USSR termed the 'next war', the Great Patriotic War, being reserved for snipers, paratroopers, combat engineers and scouts (*razvedchiki*).

Aircraft

The official end of the First World War in November 1918 did not see the sudden and total disappearance of camouflaged aircraft. German aircraft continued to fight in warpaint against Bolshevik forces in the new country of Lithuania until late 1919, but in the following year its air force largely ceased to exist under the terms of the Treaty of Versailles. In the east another new country, Poland, was fighting to establish its borders against the USSR and would use aircraft seized from Germany, still in camouflage, as well as aircraft supplied by France also in their wartime schemes. The newly created USSR would likewise use German aircraft seized along its eastern borders in this conflict, which ended in 1921. Well before Hitler came to power in 1933, Germany had begun militarisation. Clandestinely and with the help of an unlikely ally, the USSR, Germany had begun to train its pilots from 1923 onwards, and away from prying eyes in Lipezk, the Soviets, in turn, received technical assistance. The Soviets also helped in German tank development. After the relaxation of the Armistice terms under the Paris Agreement in 1926, Germany's aircraft industry, ostensibly building commercial aircraft, became as modern as that of any other country. This accelerated vastly after 1935 when Hitler revoked the Versailles Treaty.

War would also be a factor in the 1930s, with a war between Japan and China beginning in 1932 later developing into a full-scale war in 1937. Both sides would use camouflaged aircraft and tanks. The Spanish Civil War began in 1936, Germany and Italy supplying the Nationalist (Francoist) forces and the Soviet Union sending material to the Republic. German fighter aircraft of the Legion Condor appeared in an upper surface splinter scheme of two dark greens designated RLM 70 and RLM 71 (RLM standing for *Reichsluftfahrtministerium*, the German air ministry), with the undersides of aircraft painted in pale blue RLM65. German bomber aircraft arrived in the then standard bomber colours of dark brown RLM 61, medium green RLM 62 and pale grey RLM 63, this scheme being abandoned for the simpler RLM 70/71 scheme at the beginning of the Second World War and continuing as the standard bomber finish until the end of the war. Italian aircraft were supplied to the Nationalist forces in factory-applied two- or three-colour upper-surface schemes. Although Soviet aircraft arrived in the standard olive green finish, this was often mottled on arrival in Spain with light brown to blend better with the Spanish landscape.

Until the Munich Crisis of 1938, by which time the camouflaging of RAF aircraft was being introduced, the force's fighters flew with polished metal engine cowlings and aluminium painted wings and fuselages. The exception was the small force of heavy bombers that flew in an overall dark green finish known as NIVO (Night Invisible Varnish Orfordness – Orfordness being a defence establishment) developed between the wars and designed to protect a bomber against detection by searchlight. Similarly, Britain's ally France had only a small section of its aircraft camouflaged (heavy bombers) until the Munich Crisis, after which instructions were issued in December 1938 for all new combat aircraft to be finished at the factories in a disruptive pattern of khaki green, blue-grey and chestnut, the undersides of aircraft being painted grey blue. The particular manner of painting being left, it seems, to the discretion of the individual factory so there was little conformity in patterns. Bomber aircraft remained in their pre-Munich overall dark green or brown tones, with naval aircraft being finished in grey-blue upper surfaces.

US aircraft between the wars retained Olive Drab while others were in natural metal. Vulnerable training aircraft were given yellow wings and tails and bright blue fuselages. Large squadron markings were also to be seen. In addition, the 1930s saw considerable experimentation with temporary, washable camouflage finishes in three or more upper-surface colours. These could be applied according to the terrain where an aircraft operated. This concept would reappear in the Second World War with the design of the camouflaged jungle suit. The experiment with aircraft temporary finishes ended in 1940 with the introduction of a permanent and standard finish of Olive Drab for upper surfaces and Neutral Gray for under surfaces.

In the colours typical of Italian-supplied aircraft, this Nationalist (Francoist) Fiat CR.32 fighter is preserved in the Spain's national aviation museum.

Military Vehicles

Britain, for its mechanised forces, introduced between the wars a standard Dark Bronze Green, then replaced this with Khaki Green No. 3, to be replaced in the Second World War by the Standard Camouflage Colour No. 2 Khaki Brown. A sand colour had been in use in tropical countries such as India and Palestine and would remain in use into the conflict.

The USSR retained a standard olive green for its military equipment, and in this finish material would be issued to the Republican forces in the Spanish Civil War. Italian tanks destined for the Nationalists were delivered in an Italian army two- or three-colour finish. Germany's tanks to Franco were painted in a 'cloud' pattern of earth yellow, brown and green, Germany having adopted a 'cloud' scheme before the Second World War of three colours: dark green, brown and grey for home use, the green colour being later dropped. Just before the outbreak of the Second World War Germany opted for a dark grey colour, considered appropriate for the concealment of tanks and other military vehicles in the shadows of buildings or woodland. After the First World War France retained its wartime camouflage schemes; however, in its 1934 war with Cherifian forces in Morocco, French armoured cars delivered in olive green were given a reticulated pattern of ochre to blend with their desert surroundings. As with its aircraft, America had plans to adopt camouflage for vehicles according to their theatre of operations, but like the temporary aircraft finishes this concept never materialised, Olive Drab remaining supreme.

An infantry 7.5 cm leIG 18 howitzer painted with the Wehrmacht's three-colour pre-war scheme.

Military Installations

In 1931, France established a Section Permanente de Camouflage where the skill was considered an 'affair of sculpture and form, with paint secondary'. Research could be conducted in a time of peace where experimentation could be carried out using on-site observation together with sketches and scale models, achieving a high level of sophistication. The scale models could be studied under different light conditions and, when executed on site, studied from the air. The object was not to make the object disappear entirely: often the enemy would be fully aware of operations, such as the building of Maginot forts close to the German border but rather to make its precise position uncertain. An example of the attention paid by the French to the subject is the marine artist Pierre Gatier's work at the new Batterie Mèdes in 1931, situated on the Isle of Porquerolles close to the Mediterranean naval base of Toulon. France had

A casemate of the Maginot *ouvrage* of Agaisen, moulded, textured and coloured to blend with the scenery of the Alpes-Maritimes.

become concerned by the rise of Fascist Italy and had begun defence works in the Mediterranean in the early 1930s. The Dardanelles campaign in the First World War showed that ships were vulnerable to effective coastal battery fire and lessons as to their protection had been learnt from the fighting at Verdun where concrete-reinforced forts had resisted the enemy. Gatier made a detailed study of the colours of the local rocks and the local vegetation. The use of rounded forms avoided tell-tale shadows. Camouflage materials had to resist gun blast and a *treillage ceramique* (clay-coated wire mesh) was used to create forms resembling rock to cover, for example the battery's large rangefinder. New paints were required to resist the strong sunlight, the new works being painted in grey-green and light and dark chestnut. The result was highly effective the rangefinder 'rock' being still difficult to see from the sea. The work 'required the application of diverse sciences', costing only 3 per cent of the entire battery. In the mountainous Alpes Maritime, the Maginot forts built to protect France's

Clad with stone to resemble local buildings, this British machine gun post was built to defend possible landing places on the island of Malta in the 1930s.

Defences under construction in Switzerland, vulnerably situated between France, Italy and Germany. The blockhouse has been given a four-colour disruptive pattern.

border with Mussolini's Italy were made of concrete using plastic and textured designs painted to resemble rock outcrops.

Britain was also alarmed by developments in Italy. Following the Abyssinian crisis in 1935 a number of concrete machine gun blockhouses were built on the island of Malta to protect potential landing places, their exteriors being covered in stone to blend with local architecture of rubble limestone. In the Second World War, tanks based on the island would be given a reticulated pattern of green lines over sand in order to resemble the island's walls, and even infantry steel helmets were given a similar treatment. This security was necessary as Italy made plans to invade the island in 1942. Elsewhere in the empire, the 6-inch guns and shields of Sphinx Battery at Singapore, for example, were given a disruptive, jigsaw-like camouflage.

In 1936, British military observers at German military manoeuvres were put on notice when they witnessed camouflage discipline in the painting of the country's tanks and the use of *Zeltbahn* as concealment from aerial observation. The world prepared for another world war...

3

The Second World War

On 31 August 1939, Germany launched a false flag operation, an assault on the German radio station at Gleiwitz on the Polish border, camouflaged to appear as though carried out by Polish saboteurs, and one of several incidents designed to give Germany an excuse to launch its attack on Poland on 1 September 1939.

The Development of the Science of Camouflage

This war would be the first where camouflage uniforms would be worn on a considerable scale, albeit for special formations. Its wear betokened authority and acted as the badge of elite formations, such as the British Parachute Regiment. Science and art would combine as never before to study concealment. But at the beginning of the Second World War the British army had no established camouflage organisation, although Military Training Pamphlet No. 26 'Notes on Concealment and Camouflage' had been issued in 1939. In 1940, the British Expeditionary Force sent to France had no camouflage materials and had to establish a factory at Rouen to make nets, using local female labour. Gradually, a momentum developed with further training pamphlets and Army Council instructions being issued about camouflage. For example, in 1941 Military Training Pamphlet No. 46 Part 4A was issued on the painting of mechanised transport. In the same year Military Training Pamphlet No. 46 Part 2 appeared on the camouflaging of field defences. The general observations in this held good for all combatants. These were that vehicle and even foot tracks should not be visible from the air, that any natural materials used must match the background, and that shadows be avoided by for example by the use of netting, these covering the object and gradually sloping down to ground level. Defence works such as pillboxes should merge with their backgrounds and shine should be avoided, especially off roofs or off trench works – a common method to cut down on shine and to disrupt the flat shape of British pillboxes was to attach turf to their roofs. Any scheme had to avoid regularity and be as close to its background as possible; for example, a pillbox built into a hedge or by a tree. Tell-tale loopholes to be obscured by, say, metal gauze panels or by disruption, such as the painting of an irregular dark area around

A day by the sea. A rare snapshot taken on the North Wales coast showing a pillbox disguised as a refreshment kiosk. (Courtesy of the Roden family)

the loophole camouflage. Where a pillbox could not be blended into an existing feature, whether natural or an existing building, then realistic disguise and even misdirection was essential; for example, a pillbox painted to resemble a seaside kiosk with appropriate signage such as 'Teas and Ices'.

Although the military might have got off to a slow start a momentum had developed elsewhere with the establishment in 1939 of the Civil Defence Camouflage Establishment based in the Midlands town of Leamington Spa. Employing 230 staff at its peak (it was disbanded in 1944), it included many who would have distinguished careers post-war. Among these were artists such as Julian Trevelyan and Colin Moss. The headquarters were in the Regent Hotel and the Loft Theatre was requisitioned for land-based camouflage development, while the town's art gallery served somewhat later as the centre for naval camouflage. The government was aware that, by aerial reconnaissance, Germany had details of the locations of important installations, so these could not be hidden. The job of the artist/*camoufleur* was to endeavour to confuse an enemy pilot flying at a minimum of 5 miles distant from the target and at 5,000 feet in daylight conditions. Artists as well as architects were chosen because of their understanding of scale, colour and tone. Designs attempted to make a structure blend with its surroundings or deceive the eye as to the object's size and location when viewed from a warplane against a shifting background. Disruptive patterns were to be a mixture of dark and light painted areas in order to break up the shape of the object. Some vulnerable sites were difficult to conceal. The cooling towers of power stations were sometimes given elaborate painted schemes; the National Paint Federation had produced fourteen colours for the disguising of buildings. Steam from these was a problem and tests were carried out to darken this. A cheap and effective method of hiding the shadows of factory gabled roofs was the use of netting or vegetation and false structures. The town's ice rink had also been requisitioned in 1939 and in this open area technicians worked on a scale models placed on turntables and with moving lights to simulate lighting at different diurnal periods and weather conditions. A viewing platform was built in order to simulate a view from an aircraft. In addition to paint, research was carried out into paint substitutes using oil waste products and other waste products, such as shredded rubber.

The surrealist artist Roland Penrose, a Quaker and pacifist, was one of a number of people, some of whom had served on the Republican side in the Spanish Civil War, who involved themselves in defence matters, instructing under the writer Tom Wintringham at the unofficial Home Guard training school at Osterley Park. Penrose put his artistic expertise at the service of his country, eventually becoming an army captain in charge of

The elaborate, painted camouflage scheme as viewed from the powerhouse of the Ford factory at Dagenham in Essex as recorded by the war artist Helen McKie. (Courtesy of the Ford Motor Company)

34

Camouflage netting, correctly positioned to blend with local vegetation, Tunisia. A Wehrmacht 15 cm FH18 field howitzer in action photographed by war correspondent (*Kriegsberichter*) Scheffler.

the Eastern Command Camouflage Training School in Norwich, and at the Camouflage Development and Training Centre at Farnham Castle in Surrey. To startle his audience at lectures it is said that he would include a surrealist touch: a colour photograph of his future wife, the photographer and model Lee Miller, lying naked on a grassy background, covered in green camouflage cream and underneath a light camouflage net. Penrose also published in 1942 the *Home Guard Manual of Camouflage*. In this he re-emphasised the importance of background texture and colour, recommending suitable camouflage tones such as a dull earth colour, yellow and browns and greens, brick red, neutral grey and black to imitate shadow and provide a disruptive pattern, especially when running through loophole positions. The book also suggested ways of making camouflage suits using hessian painted in a disruptive pattern with the recommended colours above (if available). At Farnham too was the naturalist Hugh Cott, who in 1940 published the monumental work *Adaptive Coloration in Animals.* His spell there was short and he moved to the Cairo Camouflage Directorate. Another artist drawn into the study of camouflage was the theatre designer Oliver Messel, whose expertise was drawn on to suggest varied and appropriate schemes and materials for the camouflaging of the thousands of pillboxes being built in 1940.

A gun house at Studland Bay, Dorset, part of a 4 inch coastal artillery battery, exhibiting painted camouflage to blend with the local red sandstone.

A building on the Second World War Rhydymwyn mustard gas factory in Flintshire photographed in the 1990s and showing its original camouflage.

These included chicken wire for the attachment of foliage, and green-painted metal gauze, of the type used to replicate foliage in stage sets, cut and shaped to disguise a pillbox. His crowning achievement is said to be the Lady of Fakenham, a *papier mâché* construction resembling an eighteenth-century baroque statue situated by a strategic road junction outside the Norfolk town. On the approach of the enemy, the statue's legs would have opened to reveal a cannon.

Another artist made a reappearance: Norman Wilkinson, who this time applied himself to the camouflaging of factories and airfields. Taking a contrary point of view, he felt that the enthusiasm for camouflaging these in elaborate schemes early in the was not borne out by the results. He felt that such measures were of limited use and consumed a vast amount of time and paint. From the air a building appears in one tone, but a close view revealing camouflage would indicate a military building, so giving the game away. There followed a scaling down of elaborate designs and a trend to the use of single dark colours for large structures such as aircraft hangars. This was justified as after 1940 the Luftwaffe had begun to switch to night bombing. Additionally, in daylight or moonlit conditions many targets could be identified by natural features such as rivers or reservoirs. Furthermore, advanced German bomber navigation aids freed aircrews from the need for close observation. Of more use would be decoys: in late 1939 the Air Ministry had set up a decoy department headed by a Colonel Turner. At first realistic replicas of strategic sites such as aircraft factories were built by technicians from Elstree Film Studios. These would be located several miles from the real target but in the line of a bomber's likely course. Some, such as the Boulton and Paul dummy aircraft factory near Wolverhampton, drew enemy attacks. With the switch to night bombing these expensive sites became superfluous. Instead, night bombing 'Q' sites were built to replicate lighting effects, such as those of a marshalling yard under semi-blackout conditions (QL), with the resulting fires following a successful

This Robin aircraft hangar, photographed during the war at RAF Shawbury, was correctly situated close to a tree. In addition, it was painted to resemble local houses, even having a false chimney.

raid replicated by fire effects (QF). Naturally, with the Allied bombing campaign Germany would also follow suit, but with the country under constant aerial reconnaissance the sites were quickly discovered. But with Germany inextricably trapped in its war with the Soviet Union bombing attacks on Britain diminished significantly after 1941 and the need for elaborate camouflage was relaxed from 1943 onwards.

The USA issued a series of training manuals about personal concealment and the USSR issued written guidance. In fact, the Red Army attached great importance to *maskirovka*, as they termed camouflage. In the planning of the great 1944 offensive against German forces in the Soviet Union, 'Operation Bagration', aircraft were directed to test the effectiveness of the army's concealment measures. For maximum surprise, forces moved only at night and tanks, men and equipment remained in forests with access roads covered by overhead nets. In the Battle of Kursk in 1943 a German commander, von Mellenthin, not used to saying anything good about the Red Army, praised the thoroughness of the Soviet camouflaging of minefields and gun positions. Germany issued information in the form of *Denkschrift*.

A photograph from a 1943 US War Department Technical Manual demonstrating the effectiveness of snow camouflage.

Uniforms

Britain, unlike the countries mentioned in the previous chapter, had not developed a specific camouflage uniform pattern before the Second World War. Its infantry was issued with a khaki rubberised rain cape, with a rarer version printed in a disruptive pattern of green and brown. Likewise, the issued gas protection clothing was also given a brown and green pattern. Green helmet nets were issued as well as face veils, the latter camouflaged in a similar manner to the previous items. The popular (in cold weather) leather jerkin was given a light spray of green to tone down the tan of the leather.

The beginning of the issue of British camouflage clothing began with the design of a smock for paratroopers. Designed by a Major Denison in late 1941, possibly at Leamington Spa, the four-pocket, pull-over smock was firstly made from cloth andhand-painted with dye in various tones of green and brown. The application of a wet brush produced a diffuse coloration, a dry brush a more hard-edged pattern, and so the brush stroke pattern was born. Another hand-painted camouflaged garment was the SOE (Special Operations Executive) jumpsuit and padded helmet to give concealment to agents on landing in enemy territory, the suit being large enough to fit over civilian clothes and with pockets to contain a knife, pistol, small spade (to bury the suit and parachute). The expansion of the Parachute Regiment and the need for ever more uniforms led to a standardised brush stroke pattern being developed which was machine printed onto cloth. In the last two years of the war a two-piece windproof suit, also printed in a brush stroke pattern, was widely issued to infantry fighting in north west Europe and was also issued to the SAS with which regiment it is commonly associated. A final item of brush stroke printed clothing was the overall issued to tank crews. Cut in an identical fashion to the windproof suit was a two-piece suit in white cloth for snow conditions; it is believed that Britain supplied these to US forces in the Ardennes campaign of winter 1944–45.

A 1942 example of the British Denison Smock showing the first, and literal, Brushstroke pattern.

Also applied by hand was the camouflage of the SOE agent's jumpsuit.

For its operations in the Pacific the US Marines Corps introduced a dedicated pattern in July 1942 christened Frog Skin by its wearers. Trials of a suitable camouflage pattern were held at Fort Belvoir in Virginia under the direction of Lt Col Saint-Gaudens, the son of a sculptor and who had served in the American Camouflage Service in the First World War. Both science and art – and a touch of Hollywood – were applied to the project. The spotted, reversible pattern was designed by a noted civilian horticulturalist and writer, Norvell Gillespie. One side was predominantly green ('jungle'), the other brown ('beach') The uniform itself was also required to be insect and thorn proof, using a material called Herring Bone Twill (HBT) but in service, despite the efficacy of the camouflage pattern, it proved to be too heavy when wet. In addition, the very first uniforms were one piece, impractical for use in areas where intestinal complaints would be prevalent. A two-piece suit was then issued in mid-1943 but this still suffered from the heaviness of the HBT material. Its use was almost entirely in the Pacific although it was supplied in limited numbers to the US army in time for D- Day but quickly dropped because its pattern was felt to be too similar to those worn by the Waffen-SS. Eventually a lighter, green poplin uniform was issued for the Pacific theatre, but Frog Skin continued in use as helmet cover material and in the form of a rubberised shelter quarter. The US armed forces also made use of face camouflage creams and helmet nets.

The British army windproof uniform was machine printed in a Brushstroke pattern. This example was modified post-war, given a zip, so forming part of the uniform of the SAS.

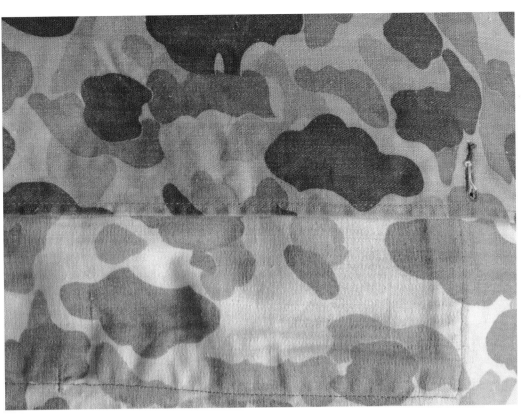

The jungle and beach patterns of the US Frogskin uniform. This Second World War example was not truly reversible.

US paratroopers were issued with a jump suit in a light khaki colour, often seen daubed with OD to darken the uniform for night operations in Normandy in June 1944. Members of the elite US First Special Service Force received a reversible parka (olive drab and white). Otherwise, most of the country's soldiers fought in Olive Drab.

The USSR, as we have seen, designed a camouflage suit in the so-called Amoeba pattern before the start of the Second world war and was supplied to specialists such as snipers (male and female), combat engineers and scouts (*razvedchiki*). In approximately 1943 was introduced a new design in a leaf pattern, which may have used existing clothing printing rollers. Again, there was a winter and a summer colour variant. The Soviets incorporated a veil into the hood of their suits to cover the face, a prominent light area. Another suit consisted of bundles of raffia strips tied or sewn onto a green fabric to break up the outline of the wearer and to blend with grass and foliage. The fact that this was rarely observed might indicate that it was impractical as the strips quickly degraded. Towards the end of the war a further pattern appeared, a stepped green pattern (resembling modern pixelated patterns) overprinted with a brown amoeba pattern. Unlike other nations, soviet paratroopers used standard Red Army uniforms, including the amoeba suit, and even jumped in greatcoats! For snowy conditions, a white suit was, naturally, part of the winter equipment. Soviet camouflage uniform research was part of the army's reliance on *maskirovka*.

Introduced in the final years of the Second World War was this Romanian-manufactured example of a Soviet leaf pattern.

In the previous chapter we saw that Germany had been early to introduce an item of camouflage clothing, the *Zeltbahn*, the pattern of which would remain largely constant until the end of the war. The Waffen-SS developed several different patterns as we also saw in the last chapter. All these patterns would also be seen on the padded uniforms (initially mouse grey and reversible to white) issued in the middle of the war for winter protection in the fighting in the East, as well as a modified splinter pattern introduced towards the end of the war, and which had a less angular and more diffuse representation of the splinter pattern, known to collectors as the Marsh Pattern. The Luftwaffe's parachutists, the *Fallschirmjaeger*, were issued with a jump smock in a pattern similar to the Wehrmacht's splinter pattern but using smaller motifs. The Luftwaffe's late war field formations also used a combat jacket in this pattern. Although a helmet cover in a splinter pattern was issued to Wehrmacht soldiers there were probably never enough of these, so soldiers would make covers from old *Zeltbahn,* from sacking or would use wire tied to a helmet onto which foliage could be attached.

The last German design was the *Leibermuster* ('body pattern'), apparently its official name. It was designed by Professor Schick, who as we have seen was active in designing the Waffen-SS patterns, but in this case the pattern would have had universal issue, replacing all other German camouflage garments. It was manufactured using special light absorbing dyes to counter detection by infra-red devices (the Germans had developed

Mail from home. Wehrmacht soldiers wearing the newly issued two-piece padded reversible (to mouse grey) uniform, one of whom has white-washed his helmet. Above the right-hand soldier, who wears the ribbon of the Iron Cross Second Class, is a *Zeltbahn*.

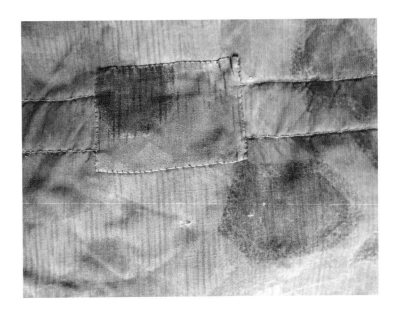

The Wehrmacht Marsh pattern, here showing two variations.

these at the very end of the war) and very few were issued. It was a pattern unlike any other German type, the addition of patches of carbon black not only giving good infra-red protection but adding sharpness to the pattern for better disruption. Larger printing rollers enabled a more random pattern to be produced, further aiding disruption. Switzerland's post-war camouflage uniform, the TAZ57, was closely modelled on the *Leibermuster* design. It is said that the red in the pattern blended well with the poppies in Swiss meadows, but it would equally be useful in brick rubble!

As an aside, Germany took over large stocks of clothing from the armies of occupied countries, much of which was khaki coloured. Not wishing to waste these uniforms and in order to provide for its massively expanding forces, these were in the greys of the Wehrmacht. Uniform details, such as pockets and epaulettes, were also re-tailored.

France did not develop a camouflage uniform before the Second World War. Alpine troops were issued with a white helmet cover for winter use but otherwise there was little in the way of snow camouflage. In the bitter winter of the Phoney War (1939–40) French patrols in no man's land were reduced, in at least one instance, to requisitioning white linen garments from convents. Ironically, the last soldiers fighting in Berlin in 1945 and wearing Waffen-SS camouflage were French volunteer members of the 'Charlemagne' Division.

The previous chapter covered the ground-breaking development by Italy of a camouflage pattern for uniform items, the *Telo mimetico*, and its subsequent use by both Italian and

The post-war Swiss TAZ57 pattern, very similar to the German *Leibermuster* pattern.

German special units. This would be the longest-lived camouflage pattern in service. As a mountainous country Italy had *Alpini*. Those sent to fight in the snows of the Eastern Front were not saved by a provision of white clothing; the *Monte Cervino* Battalion, its light support weapons frozen, disappeared in 1943. Japan was another country where camouflage clothing had not been developed, but its soldiers were resourceful in using local vegetation as capes or attaching this to helmets.

Aircraft

The wartime British Ministry of Aircraft Production issued disruptive camouflage patterns according to the size of the aircraft, with distinct divisions between colours, and with factories painting on the camouflage, patterns from aircraft to aircraft. The instructions were very detailed, giving specifications for paints and dopes (cellulose paint), durability standards and charts showing measurements from key points on a particular type of aircraft so that the pattern divisions could be chalked on for the spray painters. The USA and Germany followed similar procedures at their aircraft factories. The upper surface colours of Dark Earth and Dark Green, introduced in April 1937, represented light and dark land masses respectively, the pattern being called the Temperate Land Scheme.

An RAF Hawker Hurricane IIa fighter in the markings of the time of the Battle of Britain showing off its disruptive camouflage.

An Avro Lancaster bomber in standard RAF Bomber Command night bomber finish.

Lower surfaces were painted in a duck egg green colour called Sky. The lower surfaces of bombers, now in the green and brown scheme, were matte black to defeat detection by enemy searchlights. Black was also introduced later in the war for the undersides of RAF Lysander aircraft used on clandestine night SOE flights into Europe. For aircraft overflying the sea such as aircraft of the Royal Navy, the reconnaissance and torpedo bombers and anti-submarine aircraft of Coastal Command a Temperate Sea Scheme of Dark Slate Grey and Extra Dark Sea Grey for upper surfaces was introduced in 1939. As the bitter war in the Atlantic intensified, RAF and certain naval aircraft had, gradually, much of their lower surfaces painted white to better blend with Atlantic skies. In time the proportion of white increased to such an extent that the disruptive scheme was largely abandoned, replaced by a narrow area of Extra Dark Sea Grey.

Although disruptive patterns remained largely the same, operational changes led to the substitution on fighter and day bomber aircraft of Medium Sea Grey instead of Dark Earth, this taking place from May 1941. This reflected a move to a more offensive and over-water posture for the RAF. The fighting in the Western Desert and Mediterranean saw the introduction in August 1941 of the Tropical Scheme with Middle Stone (a sand colour) replacing the green of the Temperate Scheme, and, to reflect brighter skies, a new under surface colour of Azure Blue was issued. One little-seen camouflage scheme was an all-over white finish for RAF Meteor jet fighters serving with No. 616 Squadron in north-west Europe during the last winter of the war. At the other end of the colour spectrum, night fighters were initially painted a sooty black, This matte finish degraded

Above: A Bristol Blenheim IVF fighter painted in the RAF's green and grey scheme.

Below: The RAF Tropical Scheme as shown on a US-supplied Curtiss P-40 aircraft.

Its white camouflage besmirched by heavy use, an RAF Sunderland flying boat shows only narrow patches of Extra Sea Grey on the upper fuselage and wings.

the already inadequate performance of many of the night-fighter aircraft and was replaced from October 1942 by an all-over coat of Medium Sea Grey, with Dark Green applied in a disruptive pattern on the upper surfaces. At night, the sky is never entirely black, and the black finish had been found to give an unwanted silhouette to the fighters, so the lighter colours were quite appropriate. Another innovation related to the painting of high-altitude photo reconnaissance aircraft. After testing various colours, including pink, the RAF chose a medium, cerulean blue known as PR (Photo Reconnaissance) Blue: above forty thousand feet the sky darkens due to the thinness of the atmosphere and a light blue is ineffectual. In the closing months of the war, with little Luftwaffe opposition newly supplied Spitfire and US-supplied Mustang fighter aircraft dispensed with camouflage paint, a practice already adopted by the US Army Air Force. This bestowed benefits in terms of both weight (of the paint) and streamlining.

We have seen that just before the outbreak of war France adopted a three-colour disruptive upper surface scheme. No official guidance was given as to the shape and size of the patterns and each aircraft factory adopted its own schemes. The use of poor-quality paint or inadequate surface preparation was often apparent: bomber aircraft from the Lioré et Olivier factory often quickly exhibited paint loss, which lead to the compromising of their camouflage effect. French naval aircraft were finished in an upper surface scheme of grey blue.

Despite a non-aggression pact both the USSR and Germany were preparing for war, the Soviets in the belief and hope (the country was in the throes of a major re-equipment

50

French Bloch MB 174 reconnaissance bombers in the three-colour upper-surface colours of brown, green and grey. A propaganda postcard issued by the Vichy government.

An all-black Soviet air force Ilyushin Il-4T torpedo bomber awaits its torpedo on an airfield in the far north of Russia.

programme) that war would come in 1942. Until then Stalin wished to give the impression of a peaceful neighbour, trade continuing between the countries until the outbreak of war in June 1941. Soviet aircraft, many obsolete and in a natural metal finish, were drawn up on airfields close to German occupied territory, clearly visible to German reconnaissance aircraft, their general lack of camouflage being that of a' peaceful neighbour'. Aware in the summer of 1941 of the possibility of German aggression instructions were given for the camouflaging of all aircraft by August of that year, the Soviets had previously established in July 1939 a Service for the Camouflage of the Soviet Forces but by June 1941 little had been done, mainly due to a shortage of paints. Immediately after the German attack the Committee of Defence had found that many airfields were badly camouflaged, and most aircraft were not camouflaged at all. Stalin intervened, ordering the disruptive painting of Soviet aircraft, the first factory finishes being in the matte paints AMT4 green and AMT6 black for upper surfaces, these appearing on aircraft from July 1941 onwards. A light blue-grey shade covered aircraft under surfaces. It is believed that certain aircraft built in former tractor factories, such as the Yakovlev Yak-1 fighter, may have used green tractor paint, plus the black. No standard patterns were then laid down, these being at the whim of the factory sprayer. This disruptive scheme was in use on Soviet aircraft until mid-1943. Somewhat confusingly it closely resembled the camouflage finish applied to Finnish aircraft, with which country the USSR would fight two wars. A washable snow paint, MK7, was also supplied for winter use.

Exhibited in France's principal aviation museum in Paris is a Yakovlev Yak-3 fighter aircraft of the Normandie-Niemen squadron of French volunteer airmen fighting in the USSR. It is shown in the late war grey scheme.

Possibly influenced by changes in the painting of Luftwaffe aircraft with lighter colours suitable for aerial combat, the Soviets introduced in July 1943 a disruptive pattern of two greys, one dark and the other grey blue, for its fighter aircraft: by this date the USSR was no longer wholly on the defensive. German and Soviet aircraft would now look rather similar from a distance, which suited Soviet tactics that encouraged very-close combat. In addition, and after extensive trials, it was demonstrated that the new greys made the judgment of an aircraft's distance difficult for an enemy. Drawings were issued for the painting of the new schemes on aircraft, replacing the random schemes of the past. In addition to the new fighter greys, a grey-brown colour was introduced, possibly as a result of a shortage of the green pigment chromium oxide. Now non-fighter aircraft would be seen in a three-colour disruptive pattern of green, light grey-brown and dark grey (or black if the aircraft were a medium or heavy bomber, night bombers retaining black under surfaces). Towards the war's end, all new aircraft would be finished in the two greys. The many foreign supplied aircraft, whether from RAF or US stocks, remained in their factory delivery colours.

The standard US Army Airforce (USAAF) aircraft finish was Olive Drab upper surfaces and Neutral Gray under surfaces. To improve the camouflage effect patches of Medium Green, a lighter colour, were applied to the wing and tail edges of bomber aircraft. However, under operating conditions OD faded quickly leaving the Medium Green outlining the surfaces. This was not a desired effect, and the scheme was abandoned. Aircraft employed in North Africa had upper surfaces painted in a pinkish colour known as Sand. In October 1943, the requirement that all new USAAF aircraft be camouflaged was relaxed and aircraft began to leave factories unpainted, apart from a patch of OD as a non-reflective surface immediately in front of the pilot. The switch to a natural metal finish (NMF) gave a small speed bonus although camouflaged and NMF aircraft would be seen side by side at the war's end. The exception to the rule related to night fighters and photo reconnaissance aircraft. British night fighters supplied to the USAAF in Europe under a reverse Lease Lend Agreement retained their grey and green finish but with the introduction of their own night fighter, the Northrop P-61 Black Widow, a gloss black finish was used, this also appearing on 'Carpetbagger' B-24 Liberator aircraft on covert agent-dropping missions for the Office of Strategic Services (OSS) over Europe.

As with the RAF, there was a need for a suitable finish for high-flying aircraft. These began in 1940 in respect of Lockheed's F-5 Lightning photo reconnaissance (PR) aircraft using specially developed Haze paints. Application was lengthy, and the paint quickly weathered. It was replaced by Synthetic Haze paint. Reverse Lend Lease British night fighters, such as the de Havilland Mosquito, remained in their RAF camouflage, as did RAF-supplied PR Spitfires. The US Navy's anti-submarine aircraft such as the B-24 Liberator bomber initially retained their factory Olive Drab finish but replaced the lower surface colour of Neutral Gray with white, this covering most of the fuselage as well as under surfaces. Olive Drab was later replaced by the more appropriate colour of Dark Gull Gray. In this respect they began to resemble the aircraft of RAF Coastal Command. For aircraft carrier operations Non-Specular Sea Gray was used with Light Gray for under surfaces, this being replaced in 1943 onwards by an attractive three colour counter shading scheme for Pacific operations of Sea Blue upper surfaces, Intermediate Blue (sides), and Insignia White for under surfaces. The undersides of the upward-folding wing sections were painted in the

A US Navy F6F-5 Hellcat fighter in the three-colour countershading Pacific scheme.

A Junkers Ju 88 in a standard factory finish of two greens. The presence of yellow paint identifies the location as Russia where this colour identified Axis aircraft in order to avoid friendly fire.

Intermediate colour to blend with the carrier deck surface. With the US Navy all powerful in the Pacific a simplified finish was introduced in 1944 of overall glossy Midnite Blue.

Germany's air force, the Luftwaffe, entered the war with the upper surfaces of its aircraft in two low-contrast green colours in a splinter, disruptive pattern. In 1940 many fighter aircraft began to exhibit a lighter appearance, possibly from air combat experience over Poland in 1939. Shadow shading was adopted with the sides of the fuselage and under surfaces in the pale blue colour RLM 65 and with grey-green colour RLM 02 replacing RLM 70 black-green. A new set of colours appeared in 1941 – two greys, RLM 74 and RLM 75 – for the upper surfaces, the two colours being graduated, with RLM02 in mottles on the sides of the aircraft to achieve countershading. The Luftwaffe, apparently victorious, did not need to concern itself overly with ground camouflage yet. Bomber aircraft remained in the two greens throughout the war although towards the war's end the dark colours began to be lightened with patches of grey, with mottles or squiggles especially on night and maritime bombers and night harassment aircraft. This gave better concealment in cloud or against the sea. Night fighters, after a black interlude, adopted an all-over pale blue RLM 65 finish with mottles of grey-violet RLM 75. German's unanticipated involvement in war in North Africa and the Mediterranean called for the use of a sand colour and it is believed that paints from Italian sources were firstly used, often mottled with green to blend with the desert scrub, until the reddish sand colour RLM 79 became available. With the Luftwaffe fighting for the defence of the Reich and protection on the ground from marauding Allied aircraft now imperative, a new range of colours was introduced

A Luftwaffe Messerschmitt Bf 109 fighter aircraft photographed in northern France in 1940, its camouflage lightened by the substitution of black-green by green-grey RLM02.

Focke-Wulf FW 190 fighter bombers awaiting transfer from Poland to the Eastern Front. wearing an upper surface of the two greys RLM 74 and 75, the colours are applied in mottles to the sides as counter shading. In the background is a snow-camouflaged Junkers Ju 52/3m transport 'hack'. All red colours will be removed to avoid confusion with the red stars of Soviet fighters.

Under new management: a Junkers Ju 88 bomber, probably from an anti-shipping unit, now in the hands of the US 86 Fighter Squadron. The grey or pale blue meander pattern toned down the dark greens at sea level.

for fighter aircraft, especially the new jet and rocket aircraft, these often being hidden in woodlands and operating off autobahns. The new upper surface colours included RLM81 brown violet and RLM82 medium green. At this point in the war aircraft production was dispersed and often tail sections and wings would be painted in colours different to the rest of an aircraft. Luftwaffe squadrons, unlike their RAF counterparts, had much freedom in how their aircraft were painted, adapting them to local conditions, especially in the varied terrains of the USSR where, of course, white was applied in winter. It would be true to say that, by the middle of the war, there was little standardisation in the camouflage finishes on the force's aircraft, especially the fighter force.

Having introduced the first camouflage-printed material in 1929, it was little surprise that Italy would also camouflage its aircraft, firstly adopting in the 1930s a segmental Metropolitan scheme also employing the three colours seen in the infantry shelter quarter of green, brown and ochre. This segmental scheme was soon replaced by varied mottled patterns of green and brown superimposed over the ochre colour (*Giallo*), although sometimes this would be reversed with the base colour being green. Each aircraft manufacturer adopted its own method of applying the colours. For operations in North Africa a new colour was adopted, nut brown (*Nocciola Chiaro*), coupled with green mottles or green irregular rings to resemble desert vegetation. For the successful and daring torpedo bomber squadrons, the *Aerosiluranti,* the forward parts of their aircraft were often painted grey-blue to merge with the sky or even the sea (the aircraft flew as low as possible). The surrender of Italy in 1943 led to further changes, with those Italian aircraft fighting for Mussolini being finished in dark green. Luftwaffe-supplied aircraft remained in that service's colours.

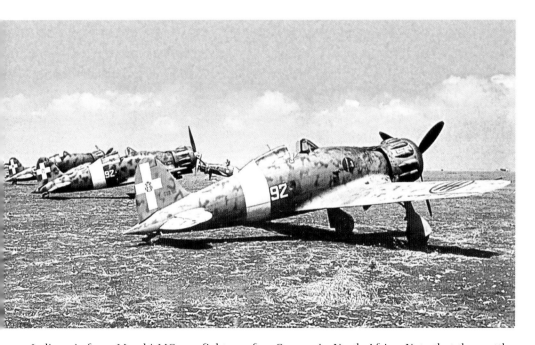

Italian air force Macchi MC 200 fighters of 13 Gruppo in North Africa. Note that the mottles vary from aircraft to aircraft, probably reflecting different manufacturers.

The Macchi MC 200 of the 21 Gruppo in Russia, these aircraft wearing a dark, mottled finish reflecting a topography different to the Mediterranean area. They have recognition markings: yellow noses and bands (German) and white triangles (Italian) on their wings to avoid friendly fire.

An Italian air force Savoia-Marchetti SM 79 torpedo bomber, its original forward camouflage over sprayed with blue grey to blend with sea and sky at extremely low operating levels.

The Japanese army and navy were entirely separate organisations pursuing their own goals. The navy's carrier borne aircraft were initially finished in grey with black lacquered engine cowlings. After the attack on Pearl Harbor in November 1941 naval aircraft adopted a standard upper surface finish of dark green with light grey below, suitable for maritime operations. The army, on the other hand, experimented with disruptive patterns on its bomber aircraft for land operations over China, then graduating to a dark green for upper surfaces, with lower surfaces often left in natural metal. As with some French aircraft, the paint wore quickly and was applied in a mottled or snake weave pattern over light grey or natural metal. The Japanese were adept at camouflaging their aircraft while on the ground using nets and local vegetation.

Military Vehicles

As with its other allies, the USA and Soviet Union, the British adopted a generally rigid system for vehicle camouflage but with some subtle changes. These changes, not always implemented, were enshrined in Army Council instructions and military training pamphlets (MTPs). A significant one was MTP No. 46 Part 4A on the camouflage painting of mechanical transport, issued in late 1941. Previous emphasis had been on painting vehicles in disruptive patterns, which was not found to be wholly effective. In the 1930s Britain had painted its vehicles including tanks in Bronze Green, but in 1939 new colours were made available for the disruptive painting: Khaki Brown No. 2 (which apparently resembled the colour of the British battle dress), Khaki Green G3 plus Dark Green No. 4. These were to be applied to tanks and other vehicles in bold disruptive stripes although variation between vehicles was stressed. Under MTP 46a emphasis was changed with the vehicle upper surfaces, including the cab and wheel surrounds, being now painted with black or Dark Brown SCC 1 to reduce shine with the risk of aerial observation, the colours being merged with the green or brown side colours in a ragged foliage-like pattern, although there was also an unofficial lobed pattern introduced called Mickey Mouse Ear. Certain vehicles including the Universal Carrier (Bren Gun Carrier) and the US supplied M3 halftrack had boxy, slab sides that begged camouflage. The former was sometimes seen in horizontal, wave-like patterns, while the US halftracks were sometimes given a Mickey Mouse ear treatment. New US and Canadian supplied tanks and vehicles after April 1944, with many British and US vehicles now in Europe, remained in their delivery colour of Olive Drab – previously they had been repainted in British schemes. It goes without saying that, under combat conditions, it was often difficult to detect a vehicle's base colour under mud, dust, foliage and net camouflage, additional armour and stores. Sometimes mud was deliberately applied in patterns; for instance, in the Tunisian desert, to lighten the dark tones of a tank.

In the Middle East a base colour called Middle Stone No. 62 was used, disrupted with a colour known as Dark Sand. An October 1942 directive of the Cairo Camouflage Directorate (one of its artists being John Hutton, the designer of the etched glass at the new Coventry Cathedral's west end) promulgated a new pattern of Desert Pink with a disruptive pattern in Olive Green. This was changed again in April 1943 with new Mediterranean and Middle East colours – SCC5 Light mud with Black or SCC 7 Green in bold designs. An additional

A British army AEC Marshall lorry with an early disruptive camouflage pattern.

desert camouflage was known as the Caunter Scheme, after its creator, and this was seen on tanks, trucks and armoured cars in the Western Desert. The colours used were Light Stone 61 or Portland Stone 64 plus Silver Grey 28 and Slate 34. These were applied in a tapering, vorticist movement-like scheme to disrupt the shape of a vehicle. Another camouflage scheme employed in the Western desert was the Sunshade Device. A canvas lorry-like tilt was erected over the turrets of British tanks and their central idler wheels were blacked out to make the whole appear to be a humble truck.

The US army painted its vehicles in the universal colour No. 9 Olive Drab. Although instructions were issued in October 1942 for the application of Field Drab No. 4 and Black the disruptive camouflage of US tanks was rare, net and foliage camouflage being more common. The US Marine Corps used its individual colour of Forest Green on its vehicles except for the LVT-4 amphibious tractors (Amtracs), widely used in the Pacific campaign, which used a naval grey colour. Unsuitable for use in jungle conditions this colour scheme was covered, when paint was available, in patches of green and brown.

France's tank manufacturers employed their own elaborate schemes using a wide variety of patterns in olive green, burnt sienna, ochre and sea green (*vert d'eau*). Black was used to outline sections of colour. One peculiarity of the French tank supply system was that specially cast turrets made in the APX foundry did not always match in colour scheme the hulls assembled in another factory, such as that of Hotchkiss. Even the famous Paris *autobus* did not escape camouflage. In 1940 these were used to transport troops, their standard green livery covered in irregular patches of French army ochre colour.

Exemplifying the cluttered appearance of many armoured vehicle is this restored US M3 halftrack in Olive Drab.

A scale model of an Austin utility vehicle painted in the Western Desert Caunter camouflage scheme.

Ton Charme
a pris mon Coeur

Ton charme a pris mon cœur: il en est tout gisse.
De toi, tout m'enchante, mais surtout tes baisers.

Still in service in 1940, this patriotic postcard shows an FT17 tank in the horizontal pattern of different colours adopted by some models of French tanks just before the Second World War.

As with its aircraft, Italy used a wide variety of camouflage patterns on its military vehicles apart from the traditional Italian grey-green. An early scheme involved a base colour of brick-red over which a green pattern was painted. In March 1941, instructions were issued for the camouflaging of vehicles in African service where the colours sand (*kaki sahariano*) and green-grey (*verde grigio*) were specified. In 1942, *terracotta* was introduced as an additional colour. No real guidelines were specified as to application it seems, this being left to the choice of individual units. Mottled and snakeskin patterns in the three colours were to be seen. Japan's tanks were painted in a three-colour scheme of willow green, brown and 'parched grass', this latter colour roughly quartering the tank when viewed from above. An earlier wartime scheme used a fourth, yellow, colour in narrow bands to form a disruptive pattern.

The dark grey colour applied to German equipment at the beginning of the war was found to be inappropriate once its forces began to be involved in the differing terrains of the Soviet Union and the Mediterranean and Western Desert, especially in areas where trees and shade was lacking. Vehicle crews had had to resort to covering their vehicles in mud to lighten the grey tone. Unprepared for a Russian winter, the Wehrmacht's armour, like the infantry, was lacking snow camouflage and resorted to expedients such as only

Mid-war on the Eastern Front. The snows have gone, replaced by mud, and *Panzergrenadiers* remove redundant whitewash from their *Sdkfz* 251 halftrack, revealing the Panzer grey colour beneath.

A three-colour finish applied to a restored *Sdkfz* 9 heavy prime mover with a Canadian Ford lorry in Olive Drab above.

A *Panzerjaeger* 38 (t) self-propelled anti-tank gun in a three-colour Wehrmacht scheme to break up the rather tall silhouette of this extemporised weapon.

A restored Wehrmacht *Jagdpanzer* 38 (t) *Hetzer* self-propelled anti-tank gun wearing the late war Ambush scheme.

Marder II 75 mm self-propelled anti-tank guns of a Panzer unit in a Russian village, their original grey camouflage now covered in mud and vestiges of whitewash.

painting with whitewash the fronts of vehicles or using white sheets. In February 1943, the Wehrmacht introduced a revolutionary new system of camouflage using a base colour, a drab sand yellow. Two other colours were supplied in pots for each tank, together with a spray gun, these being olive green and red brown, plus a smaller quantity of the yellow paint. The colours could be diluted with water or fuel, the thicker the paste, the deeper the colour. The system allowed for flexibility where differing terrains were to be encountered. In the late war period, the colours were often applied in a so-called ambush scheme where spots of all the three colours were applied to solid areas of paint to simulate light filtering through woodland. As Germany lost control of the camouflage, whether it was of paint or foliage became paramount.

Defence Installations

Early in the war Britain had set up camouflage establishments, mentioned above, which sought to instruct in the art of camouflage by courses, posters and manuals. In addition to the thousands of pillboxes other defence structures, such as coastal batteries, needed camouflage. Often the gun houses were given false fronts to resemble chalets or were netted (often the nets were garnished with scrim by women recruited from voluntary organisations). Others were painted in disruptive patterns, the colours intended to blend with the surrounding topography. The many airfields and camps built posed problems in concealment. The latter were often constructed in the parkland of country estates. Hangers, initially painted in disruptive camouflage, were eventually painted in single, dark colours. Newly built concrete runways were darkened, and bitumen used to simulate hedgerows running across the taxying ways. Airfields built during had their hangers and camps dispersed, smaller hangers could be situated near trees or near villages, even given windows and chimneys. Important works were photographed from the air to study the effectiveness of schemes. Another means of obscuring targets was the use of powerful smoke generators, although this was wind dependent.

Dwarfing the efforts of the British (one source describes their efforts as 'fancy dress') was the monumental construction and camouflaging by Germany of the Atlantic Wall. The work was carried out by the Todt organisation having unlimited supplies of both free and forced labour. much care was taken to blend the concrete coastal defences into local landscapes by the careful moulding of the reinforced concrete, by texturing and

The RAF airfield at High Ercall in Shropshire was, like all airfields, given defences against enemy air-landed troops. This machine gun post was camouflaged to resemble a shed.

The 15 cm Atlantic Wall battery at Longues-sur-Mer, Normandy, uniquely retaining its original armament. Reflecting the care with which these were built, its sculptured roof was given indentations to reduce reflection, often achieved by ramming rolled up paper into the wet concrete. This was then painted and nets were hung across the gun.

Batterie Lindemann, part of the Atlantic Wall, under construction, showing the painted camouflage scheme applied to the massive 406 mm turreted gun.

Ready for war: a monolithic air-raid shelter on Reinhardstrasse, Berlin, camouflaged to resemble a local building.

painting, and with nets always an effective shield. Care was also taken by Germany in the construction of the large air raid shelters built in major cities, these having architectural flourishes such as false windows in order to make them blend with local building styles. Provision was made for additional disguise by preparing them for brick or stone skins. The enormous flak towers in Berlin, Vienna and Hamburg, built from 1941, had their light grey concrete sides toned down with black paint to avoid their use as aiming points (they held sheltering civilians and art treasures). Although the USA was out of the range of enemy land-based bombers, factories such as the Lockheed aircraft factory at Burbank on the Pacific coast were camouflaged with nets, false buildings and even trees.

Warships

The merchant ship and warship, large objects, are difficult to conceal, this was deduced in the First World War when Dazzle camouflage was introduced to confuse and hopefully protect. In addition, a ship's wake at speed made it readily recognisable from the air, although often smokescreens could hide the wake and ship. They were extremely vulnerable to submarines and aircraft which, in the latter case, and towards the end of the war, could detect them in all weathers and even at night using air-dropped flares or airborne radar. Camouflage could only be of marginal value, but it was an asset.

68

Between the wars the British Navy painted its ships in a dark grey colour (AP507A) in home waters, in light grey (AP507C) in the Mediterranean and white in the Indian Ocean (for crew comfort, there being, at the time, little perceived enemy threat). At the outbreak of war and despite the efforts put into the camouflaging of ships in the previous war, the Royal Navy had paid little attention to camouflage, leaving commanders to choose their own schemes for their ships. For example, Lord Louis Mountbatten chose a mushroom shade for the ships of his Fifth Destroyer Flotilla by adding red to grey which was termed Mountbatten or Plymouth Pink. Despite much initial official enthusiasm, it was found that the scheme had little value and in poor light the addition of red made the ships more obvious. Other individual commanders preferred disruptive schemes which, it was thought, broke up the parabolic shape of a warship. With mounting losses in shipping the navy in 1941 had a change of heart, the Directorate of Training and Staff Duties now appointing artists and scientists to work out schemes for every ship, these being checked for effectiveness by air and sea observation. There was added confusion with such devices as painted false bow waves masking speed. With the removal of this section to Leamington Spa the operations became more scientific, the designs being tested on models in a large water tank lighted under conditions of varying visibility to simulate a ship's likely operating conditions. In 1942 a range of new paints was issued. In 1943 the Directorate of Camouflage at Leamington Spa issued a handbook explaining the nature of camouflage, the tones and paint shades to be used and the patterns employed on the myriad of smaller vessels requiring concealment. Some warships received matching patterns for port and starboard, others were given differing patterns. The work was under the direction of a

HMS *Belfast*, now moored on the Thames and wearing a Second World War Admiralty Disruptive scheme.

scientist, Alphonse Schuil, who tragically and ironically met his death when the ship he was on was sunk by a U-boat. Although disruptive patterns remained the norm, from 1941 and with Britain gaining an ascendancy over the U-boat, alternative unofficial schemes appeared. In 1940 the naturalist and naval commander Peter Scott had worked out designs for some newly delivered US destroyers and subsequently devoted much time to the study of naval camouflage. Research had shown that 67 per cent of attacks in northern areas occurred at twilight, at night or on a rising moon when a light colour was found to be more appropriate than dark grey. White or light colours were more effective in overcast conditions in the Atlantic, a factor also appreciated by the RAF, as we have seen. From 1941 a new, light-coloured splinter scheme of white, pale blue and green appeared, credited to Scott, and called the Western Approaches Scheme for use on anti-submarine warships in that zone of Atlantic operations.

Unlike aircraft or tanks, many warships enjoyed long lives and would be repainted in different schemes at regular intervals. In addition, refits might alter their appearance calling for new patterns. For example, H Class destroyers at the beginning of the war were in dark grey, then in a Dazzle type finish in 1940 of grey, black and green. From 1942 they would be seen in the Western Approaches scheme and in May 1945 in the simplified Admiralty Scheme Type B of all-over pale green with a central panel of dark blue (by this time it had been agreed that the time expended on disruptive patterns was no longer worthwhile). Smaller craft also received attention. British Vosper motor torpedo boats were given a scheme showing a false bow wave (to confuse an enemy as to the speed of the vessel) and a grey and black disruptive pattern. Another scheme involved the painting of upper surfaces in ocean blue with a grey hull, and with a white false bow wave, the pattern intended to minimise sighting at night by star shells. In the shallower waters of the

HMS *Azalea*, launched in 1940, an anti-submarine Flower Class corvette wearing a sweeping, disruptive camouflage scheme. It would later receive a Western Approaches scheme of white and pale blue.

70

brightly lit Mediterranean submarines could be detected by sight even if submerged to one hundred feet and so these craft, such as HMS *Upholder*, were given a Mediterranean Blue finish. As a rule, white was used to lighten areas in shadow. This was also used as counter shading on the lower sections of gun barrels.

In 1935, the USA had established a department for camouflage in the country's Naval Research Laboratory. Like Britain, the US would employ many varying schemes on its warships. The Fletcher Class destroyer USS *Ausburne* was first seen in solid grey with a black, false, water line, then in a grey and black disruptive scheme. In the final two years of the war, it received a patchwork scheme (termed Crazy Quilt) of greys and blacks. In the Pacific, the US Navy reinstated Dazzle to protect the many vulnerable transport ships in that theatre.

The German and Soviet navies' capital ships spent much of the war moored for safety in strongly defended harbours, the former against the power of the Royal Navy and the latter against attack by the Luftwaffe and Kriegsmarine. The use of complicated schemes was not universally seen on large German warships in the early war years. Before the Channel dash of March 1941, the battle cruiser *Gneisenau* wore a Baltic scheme of mostly dark grey with a light grey stern (to make the ship appear shorter and confuse recognition) and a false bow wave to confuse as to speed. In addition, a series of large black and white diagonal stripes were painted on the hull and superstructure: these were either part of the camouflage scheme or were air recognition features. For warships in the later war period, such as the *Tirpitz*, moored in a Norwegian fjord and vulnerable to RAF attack, a splinter

USS *Kretchmer*, a destroyer, wearing a disruptive scheme while engaged on Atlantic convoy escort duties.

A German propaganda postcard showing the battleship *Bismarck* with dark painted bow and stern plus a false bow wave, together with her Baltic service markings.

pattern of dark and light greys was employed as well as nets and even trees to make the ship appear to be part of the fjord. Smaller ships, increasingly very vulnerable to aerial attack, were often given complicated schemes of splinters, mottles and even *trompe l'oeil* patterns. Apart from the universal grey, Soviet ships also used disruptive camouflage. Japan also used grey but in the closing months of the war and, powerless against US air power, would also resort to *trompe l'oeil* to hinder and confuse recognition of its vulnerable aircraft carriers. This consisted of painting the flat decks of aircraft carriers such as the IJN *Zuiho* with false turrets and guns to make the ship, from the air, resemble a cruiser – a far less important target.

Finale

The war began with a ruthless act of deception and, with the war nearing its conclusion, Germany would carry out a further false flag operation, *Greif*, within the last-ditch attempt by Germany to halt the western Allies in the Ardennes in December 1944, Operation *Wacht am Rhein*. English-speaking commandos dressed in US uniforms and under the command of *Obersturmbannführer* Otto Skorzeney, the man who had rescued Mussolini in 1943, made their way behind US lines using captured Jeeps. Having few captured US tanks, they were supported by Panther tanks camouflaged to resemble US tanks. To do this sheet metal panels were attached to these make them resemble US M10 tank destroyers. White US recognition stars were also added to give further realism. Their goal was to carry out sabotage and create confusion and chaos behind the Allied lines. Only partially successful, the forces commandos were overcome and several SS soldiers, found dressed in US uniforms and considered as spies, were shot.

4

The Cold War and Beyond

The dire threat of nuclear warfare, ushered in at the end of the Second World War, did not bring an end to conflict, especially in respect of smaller wars. With increased mechanisation and mobility, the pace of war would change and be often far ranging. Intelligence gathering would grow beyond measure after the launch of the first satellite, Sputnik, in 1957. Aircraft retained a key role whether as high-flying spy planes such as the US SR-71 or as a means of defending airspace or attacking an enemy. Missiles, first pioneered by Germany in the previous war, assumed great importance although fighter aircraft still also relied on fast-firing cannon. The tank became increasingly vulnerable to missiles as did the warship. Reliance on computers developed but camouflage remained important. In the Vietnam War, which ended in 1975, US forces attempting to prevent infiltration along the Ho Chi Minh Trail air-dropped thousands of ADSID (Air Delivered Seismic Intrusion Detectors) sensors in order to detect movement. These had aerials that appeared to be foliage and the whole was painted in a mottled camouflage pattern to blend with the jungle. Their signals were picked up by overflying aircraft and relayed to an enormous building in Thailand holding an IBM1401 air-conditioned computer. Despite the enormous expense it was a failure.

Uniforms

In the film *A Bridge Too Far* Lt Col Frost, played by Anthony Hopkins, remarks in the centre of Arnhem, 'Something has just occurred to me. We are wearing the wrong camouflage [Denison Smock]. It's all very well in the countryside but I doubt if it will fool anyone in the town...' The right camouflage for the job was clearly called for and modern advances in computerisation and printing lead the way, as we shall see.

Germany would reprise the Splinter and Marsh patterns for the new West German army, the *Bundeswehr*, and for its border security organisation, the *Grenztruppen*, respectively. Both patterns would eventually be replaced by a grey-olive uniform, and then by *Flecktarn*, a pattern heavily influenced by the wartime Waffen-SS patterns. Other countries influenced by the Waffen-SS patterns included Egypt and Austria. Variations on the Splinter camouflage pattern would also be adopted by other countries after the war including Poland and Bulgaria, both Warsaw Pact countries. The French made use of surplus *Zeltbahn* in their war in French Indochina. In this and in the later Vietnam War the communist forces made use of captured US-supplied camouflaged parachute material, adapting them as cloaks and helmet covers. The Rain pattern seen on the *Zeltbahn* also made a return during the Cold War on Czech, Polish and East German uniforms, the latter's first large-scale issue uniform pattern being known as *Blumentarn*, patches of browns and green on a grey background.

The West and the USSR studied all aspects of German wartime research. The US, whose Marine Corps post war adopted the Mitchell leaf pattern for helmet covers and ponchos, had been impressed by the effectiveness of Professor Schick's designs commissioned a study after the war known as the Richardson Report. The infra-red and effectiveness at different ranges of *Leibermuster* were studied and, after a long delay, in 1966 the US army field trialled a pattern known as ERDL (Engineer Research and Development Laboratory), a design going back to 1948. A uniform in this pattern was issued initially to special units in the Vietnam war which, until then, had often relied on privately purchased Duck Hunter or by US 'advisers' obtaining the popular South Vietnamese army Tiger Stripe uniforms (a variation on the earlier French-supplied Lizard camouflage uniform, itself a variation

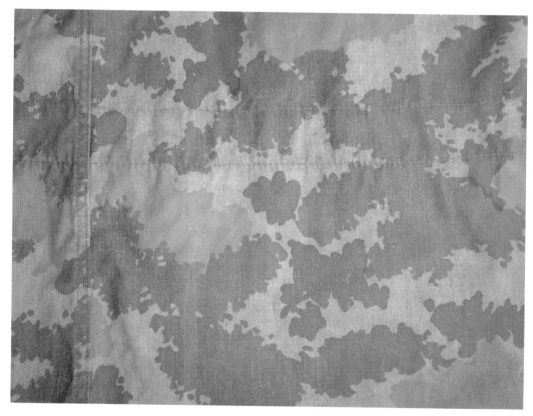

The first camouflage uniform in widespread issue to the East German Army (NVA) was one in this pattern, nicknamed *Blumentarn*.

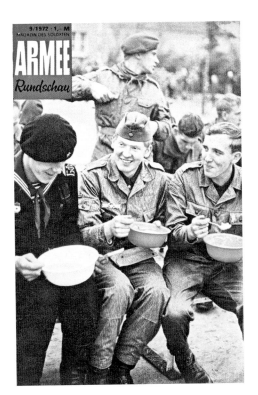

Right: Replacing *Blumentarn* was the Raindrop pattern, also supplied to separatist armies during the Cold War. Here an East German soldier is flanked by a Soviet sailor and a Pole in a low-contrast grey camouflage uniform.

Below: The present German army camouflage uniform is known as *Flecktarn,* a pattern dating from the mid- 1970s.

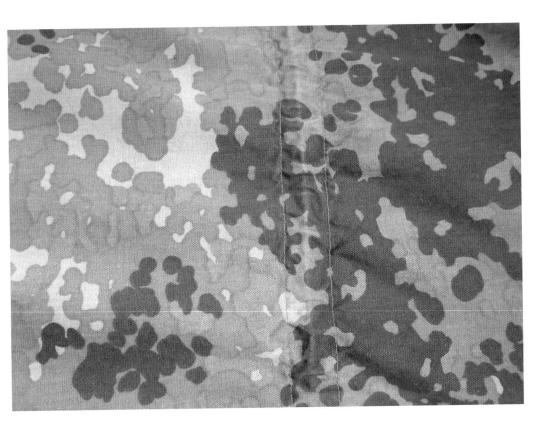

A US 'boonie' (jungle) hat in the ERDL pattern from the Vietnam War era.

of the British Denison Brush stroke pattern). ERDL proved popular and effective, and it is said that US helicopter pilots had difficulty in seeing the soldiers they were to extract from the jungle. Simultaneously Britain trialled and adopted a rather similar pattern, both patterns using areas of black for infra-red and fractal effectiveness, known as DPM (Disruptive Pattern Material), one of several Woodland patterns. This replaced other British camouflage uniform patterns including the cherished Denison Smock and that worn by the SAS, a zipped version of the wartime Windproof Smock. With the US withdrawal from Vietnam in 1975 its armies phased out the ERDL pattern and adopted the M81 Battle Dress Uniform (BDU), a Woodland pattern suitable for operations in Europe, the next likely scene of conflict. This pattern had larger motifs than ERDL and better camouflage effectiveness. Other NATO armies, such as France, would follow suit in issuing Woodland patterns. The British, German and French patterns, for example, could use similar motifs but with different colours to produce uniforms for desert use. Britain had, before its withdrawal 'East of Suez' in 1970 designed a desert camouflage uniform with a DPM pattern but, now finding these redundant, they were sold to Iraq. When Britain entered the First Gulf War in 1990 its soldiers lacked an appropriate uniform and were to be seen in the European Woodland uniform before a new desert DPM uniform was rushed to them.

The fall of the Berlin Wall in 1989, the collapse of the Warsaw Pact and new wars beginning in the Middle East and Africa made DPM and other Woodland patterns somewhat redundant.

Right: Detail of a South Vietnamese army issue shirt in the indigenous Tiger Stripe pattern.

Below: The complicated structure of the early British Disruptive Pattern Material (DPM), later much simplified.

Left: The first US desert pattern, the six-colour 'chocolate chip', was soon replaced by a simpler pattern.

Below: The Australian Army adopted a camouflage named AUSCAM. Its desert pattern variant used the colours shown including an unusual lilac shade.

The USA developed a computer designed pixelated-printed uniform in grey, the Universal Camouflage Pattern (UCP). The US Marines also had their own distinct pixelated pattern, MARPAT (Marine Pattern), in woodland, desert and urban patterns. Canada produced CADPAT, another computer-generated pattern. Despite much expense UCP was regarded as a failure, having low contrast and therefore low camouflage value, as was the US Air Force's atavistic grey, Tiger Stripe, the Airman Battle Uniform (which included in its early pattern the logo of the USAF). The USAF is now switching to the army's Operational Camouflage Pattern (OCP), suitable for use in a variety of zones, being a modified version of the commercially developed US Crye Corporation design known as MultiCam, also adopted from 2015 by the US army and other armies. The British army has also adopted a similar pattern, called MTP (Multi Terrain Pattern), itself a return to the 'universal' pattern of *Leibermuster*. For its operations specifically in the Middle East, the USA firstly adopted a five-colour uniform, christened Chocolate Chip because of its brown pebble pattern, then a simplified three-colour pattern before replacing this with OCP. In this century China has experimented with and produced a wide range of pixelated patterns for different terrains. Such computer-generated patterns can be quickly adjusted for scale and colour.

It is not clear if the Soviet Union was influenced by German camouflage research, possibly not. At the end of the war a new, stepped, green-on-sand pattern appeared, resembling modern pixelated patterns but not computer generated, with a brown lobed pattern superimposed. In the 1960s a one- or two-piece bright green and grey reversible (to light grey and green for use in semi-snow conditions) pattern emerged, also stepped, and

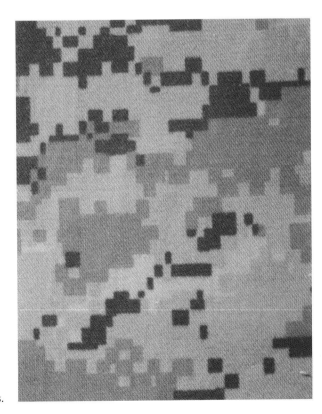

An early pixelated pattern was the US Marine Corps MARPAT. This is the woodland pattern: other colour variations catered for urban or desert environments.

The unsuccessful US Universal Camouflage Pattern (UCP) here with infra-red night-vision devices. (Courtesy of Wayne Cocroft)

used by KGB border guards, paratroopers, Spetsnaz and other special units. To collectors this is referred to as KLMK camouflage. In the 1980s the USSR also produced a Woodland pattern, of green and dark brown on a light green background. In the USSR's war in Afghanistan appeared the KZS stepped pattern printed on a loose sacking-type material in green and ochre colours and having a low reflective value. These disposable, hooded suits were also issued to specialist units. Since the fall of the USSR Russia has produced a very wide range of camouflage patterns, the present one being a green, low-contrast pixelated design.

Apart from major conflicts, the period after the end of the Second World War was marked by a series of colonial wars. In Indochina, the French fought a guerrilla war from

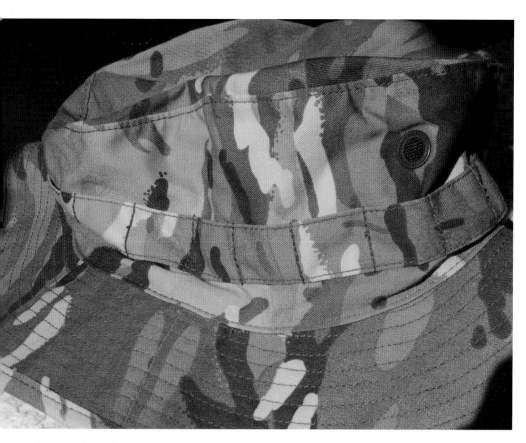

The British Multi Terrain Pattern (MTP) resembles the new US Operational Camouflage Pattern (OCP).

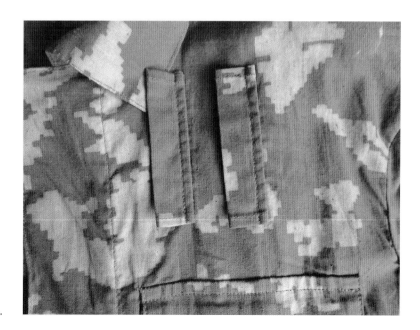

The Soviet early Cold War two-colour KLMK pattern with foliage attachment loop.

A rare example of uniform Dazzle: this pattern was adopted by Czech Warsaw Pact paratroopers.

An example of the multiplicity of Russian camouflage: internal security (MVD) uniforms in (from left to right) urban, mountain and desert patterns. (Courtesy of Dr J. F. Borsarello)

The French army issue *Bigeard* cap in Lizard camouflage. (Courtesy Amber Lowry)

1946 to 1962 with the communist Viet Minh. We have seen that both sides used war-surplus materials. France, lacking camouflage uniforms suitable for its campaign, looked to Britain and the USA. From the former it bought Denison smocks (also seen in France's war in Algeria), windproof smocks and trousers, which were termed 'sausage skins' because of the fineness of the cotton. These were often reworked, gaining zips and a degree of styling. From this material was made the iconic Bigeard cap, named after a commander of Foreign Legion paratroopers. Later issued in Lizard camouflage, it became an official item of clothing for elite units From the US they purchased Frog Skin jungle uniforms, and an individual soldier might be seen wearing items of clothing originating from both sources. The need for purchasing surplus uniforms was solved in the 1950s by the introduction of France's own brush stroke pattern known as the Lizard pattern, referred to previously, officially known as *modèle 1947/52*. In the later Vietnam war, the South Vietnamese army, which had previously worn French-supplied uniforms, remodelled the pattern, substituting black for the brown in Lizard. Another country to use Lizard was Israel, whose elite forces used surplus French uniforms in the Arab-Israeli war of 1967.

In addition to wars in Asia and the Middle East, south-west Africa was a war-torn region. Colonial wars erupted in Angola and Mozambique between liberation armies and the Portuguese, whose army used a camouflage pattern similar to the French Lizard pattern. Conflicts erupted in Southern Rhodesia (now Zimbabwe) and on the fringes of South Africa. Rhodesia adopted a brush stroke pattern, appropriately for an ex-British colony, while South African elite forces used indigenous patterns. The guerrilla armies received camouflage uniforms from Cuba and the Warsaw Pact, including large numbers printed in the East German army raindrop pattern, quite appropriate for the bush. South Africa, for its covert counter-insurgency operations, sent out scouts into enemy territory (with appropriate face camouflage) dressed in South African made copies of captured Portuguese and Warsaw Pact uniforms, especially the raindrop pattern. These conflicts lasted from the mid-1960s until the late 1980s.

Aircraft

The world war had not long finished when tensions between the East and West heightened. A Soviet blockade led to the Berlin Airlift from 1948 to 1949. In 1949, the North Atlantic Treaty Organisation was established with the USA as the major partner together with the majority of European nations, now facing the Iron Curtain. Grey and green disruptive camouflage was worn again by RAF aircraft in Europe, as well as being adopted by other European nations' aircraft. In 1950 erupted the Korean War. North Korean troops, backed by China and USSR, invaded South Korea. The United Nations rushed armed forces to aid the South. US aircraft, uncamouflaged (apart from night-bombing Boeing B-29 and B-50 aircraft, which had black undersides and carrier borne aircraft in Midnite Blue) aided hard-pressed troops. MiG15 jet fighters, piloted by Soviet advisers, often veterans of the Eastern Front, came as a shock to the UN forces. Gradually the forces of the north were forced back. Frequent US bombing attacks on North Korean airfields forced the temporary camouflage of the MiGs in a variety of patterns, including a green snakeskin pattern over natural metal and one incorporating black, sand and green mottles. British RAF aircraft remained in natural metal finish, but carrier-borne Royal Navy aircraft retained Extra Dark Sea Grey upper surfaces with Sky below.

The carrying of nuclear weapons led to special measures to protect high-flying bombers from the great heat and light of a nuclear blast. US bombers were given white reflective under surfaces, the RAF's V-bombers adopting all over white with pale roundels to cut down on destructive light absorption. However, the shooting down of a high-altitude US U-2 reconnaissance aircraft in 1960 led to a rethink on the part of the RAF. It had been assumed up to then its bombers operated above the range of Soviet anti-aircraft weapons. This was no longer the case. Consequently, the large Vulcan and Victor V-bomber aircraft were given a disruptive grey and green finish in the hope that they could now operate below the range of Soviet radars and missiles.

An East German air force Sukhoi Su-22 fighter-bomber, supplied by the Soviet Union, wearing a late Cold War temporary camouflage.

An Avro Vulcan V-bomber photographed during the period of the Cold War and wearing the grey and green disruptive finish adopted for low-level operations.

On winter operations or exercises British military aircraft often receive temporary white finishes. Here a Royal Marines Westland Sea King helicopter is wearing camouflage and the markings of SFOR during the Bosnian emergency in the 1990s.

In 1965, the USA entered another war in Asia: the Vietnam War, lasting until 1975. The military put much faith in America's overwhelming technical advantages, especially in sophisticated electronic systems and aircraft. Clandestine photographic reconnaissance flights over Laos from US bases in Thailand led to the need for the camouflaging of the McDonnell RF-101 aircraft, operating at very low level. A three-colour disruptive upper-surface camouflage called the South East Asia Pattern, also known to the US Air Force as 'Crazy Quilt', was introduced of two dark greens and tan. Under surfaces were either light grey or black. This finish was intended to give aircraft protection at a low level from observation by enemy anti-aircraft gunners but also from above by enemy fighters, and even a degree of protection on the ground from Viet Cong commando raids. Navy aircraft, operating from carriers during the war, retained Gull Grey and white, while other naval aircraft, on special reconnaissance missions received disruptive schemes of different greys. National markings were reduced in size. The conclusion of the war led to the large Boeing B-52 bombers eventually losing the tan, being given a very drab scheme in two greens and charcoal grey, known as European 1. These veteran aircraft, still operational, have now been given an all-over Gunship Grey finish, common to other contemporary USAF aircraft.

Then there were the smaller wars. For example, the Yom Kippur war of 1973 pitted Arab aircraft in sand and green against Israeli aircraft in two shades of sand and a light green. The RAF adopted a colour known as Desert Pink for operations in the Gulf Wars, as well as temporary snow camouflage in peacekeeping operations in Bosnia.

A US Phantom F4 fighter, supplied to Denmark under the terms of the NATO agreement, still retaining the three-colour Vietnam scheme in 1993.

A US air force General Dynamics F-16 Fighting Falcon in the two-tone grey scheme carried by this fighter aircraft, portrayed in 1982. Grey has now become the predominant aircraft camouflage.

The drab tones of the three-colour European 1 camouflage scheme as applied to a US B-52H heavy bomber in 1984.

A US-supplied Israeli air force F4F Phantom fighter bomber in standard three-tone camouflage.

The Falklands (Malvinas) War of 1982 war saw British Harrier aircraft in the then standard disruptive scheme of green and grey pitted against similarly camouflaged Argentinian French-supplied Dassault fighters. Argentina also employed Pucará counter-insurgency aircraft, which, originally in a natural metal finish, were given a very hasty camouflage.

And if at the beginning of the twenty-first century one might expect camouflage to be about to disappear, then look at the futuristic Northrop Grumman B-2 Stealth bomber,

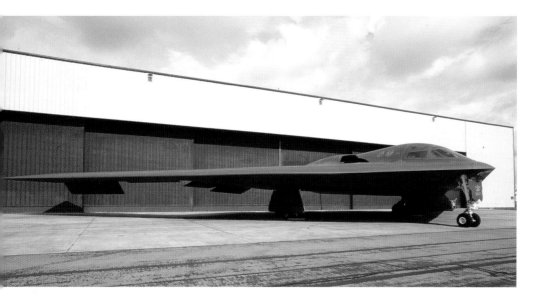

A Northrop-Grumman Spirit B-2 Stealth bomber photographed in 2019 and wearing a special grey camouflage scheme.

designed around a multi-spectral camouflage system, its rounded surfaces of a special radar absorbent material giving it a low radar signal and buried, high, rear-mounted engines reduce infra-red detection and noise. To reduce optical visibility during daylight flights the aircraft is painted in an anti-reflective grey paint. At extremely high altitudes it was found that this colour blended well with the sky. Russia, too, still employs *maskirovka*. In the latter part of the twentieth century the prototype of a new anti-tank helicopter, the Kaman Ka-50, was given false windows and doors in order to confuse as to its true operational role.

Tanks

In a return to the pre-war US wish that camouflage should match operational environments (possibly influenced by Second World War German Panzer camouflage), in the 1970s the US army introduced the complex MERDC (Mobility Equipment Research and Development Camouflage) concealment painting system. Twelve colours were specified together with fixed painting patterns. Four colour groups were used, and by minimal substitution a range of backgrounds could be covered. These included: Grey and Red Desert, Snow with Open Terrain, and Snow with Trees, Tropical Verdant, Winter Arctic, and Winter US and Europe Verdant. This system was abandoned in 1984 in favour of the standard European NATO pattern of three colours: black, red-brown and bright green. Britain retained Olive Drab broken up by a black disruptive camouflage pattern, very effective in shadows or in a wooded landscape. With the fall of the Berlin Wall and a succession of conflicts in the Middle East the tendency is now for military vehicles to be seen in sand colours, including a pink shade favoured by the SAS for their Land Rovers. Inevitably, these vehicles were called Pink Panthers or just Pinkies. However, the war launched by Russia against Ukraine may change this trend. Before the fall of the Berlin Wall the British Garrison designed an unusual urban camouflage for its tanks and support vehicles. This consisted of squares in different colours in a re-rendering of Dazzle camouflage.

The tank, becoming ever larger with up-gunning, has become more difficult to conceal and is vulnerable to ground and air-launched anti-tank missiles. Complicated camouflage schemes have become superfluous and reliance has now to be put on anti-aircraft protection systems, or by the discharge of smoke to hide these large vehicles.

Above: 4.A Soviet BRDM-1 scout car, its Soviet olive-green finish overlain with a disruptive pattern. Behind is a Second World War British army lorry, with a Khaki Green and black Mickey Mouse Ear scheme.

Left: A US army truck in the Cold War Winter Verdant MERDC scheme.

A British army Scimitar armoured reconnaissance vehicle with a disruptive pattern of a sand colour over the original Olive Drab and black finish. Additional camouflage is in the form of netting and scrim. (Courtesy of Open Govt Licence v3.0)

A Land Rover of the British army Berlin Garrison showing the Dazzle scheme applied to its tanks and transport vehicles during the Cold War.

Painted in the NATO three-colour pattern is this French Foreign Legion Jeep photographed in Calvi, Corsica in the 1980s.

Warships

The days of the large warship, so vulnerable to air and submarine attack, has now gone, the only large warships remaining are aircraft carriers, designed with aircraft, radar and missile systems to look after themselves. Other than for small, specialist craft camouflage is no longer applied: exceptions are the use by US forces in Vietnam of riverine gunships given a green and brown mottle to make them blend with the vegetation on the riverbanks, and Swedish patrol boats given a splinter pattern of colours to make them blend with the sea and the country's rocky coastline. A splinter pattern was also adopted for camouflaging aircraft as well as the country's soldiery.

HMS *Starkodder*, a Hugin Class patrol boat of the Swedish navy wearing a splinter camouflage.

Above: A Swedish Saab 37 *Viggen* also in a splinter, disruptive scheme.

Right: Appropriately for the port where many Dazzle schemes were applied in the First World War, a Mersey ferry boat was repainted in 2015 in a bright design by the artist Sir Peter Blake to celebrate the spirit of the scheme.

Bibliography

General

Hartcup, Guy, *Camouflage: A History of Concealment and Deception* (Newton Abbot: David and Charles, 1979)

Newark, Tim, *Camouflage* (London: Thames and Hudson, 2007)

Stanley II, Roy M., *To Fool a Glass Eye: Camouflage Versus Photoreconnaissance in World War II* (Shrewsbury: Airlife Publishing Ltd, 1998)

Uniforms

Beaver, Michael D. with Borsarello, Dr J. F., *Camouflage Uniforms of the Waffen-SS: A Photographic Reference* (Atglen, Pennsylvania: Schiffer Publishing Ltd, 1995)

Borsarello, J.F., *Camouflage Uniforms of European and NATO Armies 1945 to the Present* (Atglen, Pennsylvania: Schiffer Publishing Ltd, 1999)

Borsarello, J. F., *Les Tenues Camouflées Pendant la Deuxieme Guerre Mondiale* (Paris: Gazette des Uniformes, Hors Serie No. 1, 1992)

Desmond, Dennis, *Camouflage Uniforms of the Soviet Union and Russia: 1937 to the Present* (Atglen: Pennsylvania: Schiffer Publishing Ltd, 1998)

Palinckx, Werner with Borsarello, Dr J. F., *Camouflage Uniforms of the German Wehrmacht* (Atglen, Pennsylvania: Schiffer Publishing Ltd, 2002)

Aircraft

Bell, Dana, *U.S. Airforce Colours Volumes 1–3* (Carrollton, Texas: Squadron/Signal Publications, 1979, 1980 and 1997)

Bowyer, Michael J. F., *RAF Camouflage of World War 2: Airfix Magazine Guide 11* (Cambridge: Patrick Stephens Ltd, 1975)

Breffort, Dominique and Jouineau, André, *French Aircraft from 1939–1942, Volumes 1 and 2* (Paris: Histoire et Collections, 2004 and 2005)

Davis, Larry, *Gunships: A Pictorial History of Spooky* [special operations aircraft of the Vietnam war] (Carrollton, Texas: Squadron/Signal 1982)

Doll, Thomas E., Jackson, Berkley R. and Riley, William A., *Navy Air Colors: United States Navy, Marine Corps, and Coast Guard Aircraft Camouflage and Markings Vol. 1 1911–1945* (Carrollton, Texas: Squadron/Signal Publications, 1983)

Dunning, Chris, *Regia Aeronautica: The Italian Airforce 1923–1945 An Operational History* (Hersham, Surrey: Classic-Ian Allan Publishing, 2009)

Ferkl, Martin, *Japanese WWII Aircraft in Colour: Volume 1* (Ostrava-Poruba, Czech Republic: REVI Publications, 2006)

Hornat, Jiri, *Colors of the Falcons: Soviet Aircraft Camouflage and Markings in World War II* (Ottawa: Iliad Design, 2006)

Merrick, K. A., *Luftwaffe Camouflage and Markings 1935–4, Vol 1* (Melbourne: Kookaburra Technical Publications Pty, 1973)

Mondey, David, *The Hamlyn Concise Guide to British Aircraft of World War II* (London: Hamlyn, 1982)

Permuy Lòpez, Rafael A., *Air war Over Spain: Aviators, Aircraft and Air Units of the Nationalist and Republican Air Forces 1936–1939* (Hersham, Surrey: Classic Ian Allan Publishing Ltd, 2009)

Smith, J.R. and Gallaspy, J.D., *Luftwaffe Camouflage and Markings 1935-45, Volumes 2-3* (Melbourne: Kookaburra Technical Publications Pty Ltd, 1976 and 1977)

Various Authors, *Luftwaffe Colours* (Hersham, Surrey: Classic Ian Allan Publishing, various dates)

Tanks

Culver, Bruce and Murphy, Bill, *Panzer Colours: Camouflage of the German Panzer Forces, 1939–45* (London: Arms and Armour Press, 1975)

Culver, Bruce, *Panzer Colours 2, Markings of the German Panzer Forces, 1939–45* (London: Arms and Armour Press, 1978)

Culver, Bruce, *Panzer Colours 3, Camouflage and Markings of the German Panzer Forces, 1939–45* (London: Arms and Armour Press, 1984)

Vauvillier, François, *Les Automitrailleuses de Reconnaissance Tome 1 and 2* (Paris: Histoire et Collections, 2005)

Gander, Terry and Chamberlain, Peter, *British Tanks of World War 2: Airfix Magazine Guide 17* (Cambridge: Patrick Stephens Ltd, 1976)

Gander, Terry and Chamberlain, Peter, *American Tanks of World War 2: Airfix Magazine Guide 26* (Cambridge: Patrick Stephens Ltd, 1977)

Ledwoch, Janusz, *Mussolini's Tanks: Camouflage and Markings of the Italian Armored Forces from 1930 to 1944* (Warsaw: Militaria, 2006)

Wise, Terence, *D-Day to Berlin: Armour Camouflage and Markings of the United States, British and German Armies, June 1944 to May 1945* (London: Arms and Armour Press, 1979)

Zaloga, Steven J., *Blitzkrieg: Armour Camouflage and Markings, 1939–1940* (London: Arms and Armour Press, 1980)

Zaloga, Steven J., *Japanese Tanks 1939–45* (Oxford: Osprey, 2007)

Artillery and Defence Structures

Lowry, Bernard, *British Home Defences 1940–45: Fortress 20* (Oxford: Osprey Publishing, 2004)

Vauvillier, François, *Les Canons de la Victoire 1914–1918, Tome 1: L'Artillerie de Campagne* (Paris: Histoire et Collections, 2006)

Warships

Hodges, Peter, *Royal Navy Camouflage 1939–1945* (New Malden, Surrey: Almark Publishing Co. Ltd, 1973)

Stern, Robert C., *Kriegsmarine: A Pictorial History of the German Navy 1935–1945* (London: Arms and Armour Press, 1979)

Wingate, John (Series Editor), *Warships in Profile* (Windsor, Berkshire: Profile Publications Ltd, 1972)

Other Sources

- Histoire et Collections of Paris (histoireetcollections.com) publish many excellent illustrated periodicals (especially *Militaria Magazine*) and books covering the wars of the twentieth century.
- Osprey, an imprint of Bloomsbury Publishing, produce a large variety of publications at reasonable prices with colour plates. The US firm of Squadron/Signal produce well-illustrated monographs on aircraft, tanks and warships with colour plates.